Find your
"Inner Force"

The INNER FORCE

Return to the Dark Continent

By

Frank Schmitz

authorHOUSE

1663 LIBERTY DRIVE, SUITE 200
BLOOMINGTON, INDIANA 47403
(800) 839-8640
www.authorhouse.com

This book is a work of non-fiction. Names of people and places have been changed to protect their privacy.

© 2004 Frank Schmitz.
All Rights Reserved.

No part of this book may be reproduced, stored in a retrieval system, or transmitted by any means without the written permission of the author.

First published by AuthorHouse 07/20/04

ISBN: 1-4184-7503-3 (sc)
ISBN: 1-4184-7504-1 (dj)

Printed in the United States of America
Bloomington, Indiana

This book is printed on acid-free paper.

Disclaimer

This book is a journal of my African adventure along with memories of other stories and events. Although all the accounts are factual to my recollection some stories may have incorrect facts, claims or names. Many of my stories are based on memory and my recollection and could vary from some one else's recollection. I state as fact my personal opinions and beliefs as the daily events unfolded. However that does not necessarily means that my opinions were always factual or correct.

This book not only puts you on the edge of your seat while reading about the wild game stories, it is as equally exciting as it challenges you to think deeper about your own individual lives-- seeking adventure, challenges, victories and pleasure.
-Karen J. Schmitz

This is a small peak at a fun and exciting hunting career as well as a glimpse into the heart of a true woodsman and mentor. Only lucky family and friends get to enjoy a campfire chat and a few sundowners and other tales.
Tim G. Schmitz

This book is hard to put down. I found the manuscript as a whole pretty distinguished, very interesting and memorable. I'll remember the sense that you wound up in a very different world, a very dangerous world, and not just due to the presence of large wild beasts. I found your attitude to be really admirable, your natural friendliness and lack of prejudice toward the people, taking them as individuals, appreciating the way they live. Lots of adventure, with sensitivity and respect for the animals. And how frustrating and risky to have to use borrowed guns and inadequate ammo. The anger with the British really came across justified. Wow!
-Don Burgress
of the R.M.E.F
Bugle Magazine Editor

Dedication

This book is dedicated to my wife Theresa, or less formally known as Terri. She had to carry the load at our lodge and outfitting business while I laid down foot prints in Africa. She also has had to forgo vacationing on cruise ships or sunny beaches to instead sleep in tents at sub-zero weather or scale mountains with me for the past several decades. She has accompanied me on most of my adventures which has made them all the more memorable for me. I can only thank her for unselfishly always supporting my endeavors. She has helped, worked and endured more than what should ever be expected from someone in a long-standing marriage.

Thank you my companion, business partner, lover and best friend.

Acknowledgements

It's funny how certain people influence and mold your life from an early age on. These people inevitably make you into the person you become. I can only hope that my influence has been as positive on others as these people have been on myself. With that said I would like to acknowledge and thank all those folks who inspired me and molded me into who I am!

Special thanks are in order for these mentors.

My dad Francis (Cisco) who sparked the fire that burns in me to hunt, fish and dream of the next adventure. My mom Norma, who tried her hardest to keep me on the straight and narrow while growing up. Although I often tested her faith, she never gave up believing in me. My deceased uncle Nick Schmitz who inspired me at a young age to want to lead, create and build my own business. My good friend and father figure Leon Deppiesse who taught me about hard work and its rewards. My Boy Scout leader Bob Arndt and Jack Schoeller whom kindled my interested in camping and being active in the outdoors. My grandpa and grandma, Pat and Rose Tackes for having a farm for me to go visit. A place to wonder, explore and develop a love for animals. These folks molded me and inspired me as well as many others.

Thank you all.

Most of all a royal thank you is due for my beloved sister-in-law, Karen, who worked for untold hours trying to decipher and translate my scribbling and type it into words, sentences and paragraphs. Without her the words of the Inner Force may never have been heard. Also, a thank you is due to my brother-in-law Dan Wilson for editing assistance.

Table of Contents

My Adventure 1
My Journey Begins 5
People of Zimbabwe 29
The Hunt Begins - June 1 33
June 2 45
June 3 53
June 4 65
June 5 73
June 6 85
June 7 97
June 8 121
June 9 137
June 10 155
June 11 169
June 12 177
June 13 - The Inner Force 187

My Adventure

Africa is a place that stretches one's imagination for those that have been there and for those that have not! Visions of Africa dance in everybody's heads, but only a few lucky people understand reality from fiction. The lucky few that have been there, tasted, touched and seen the mysteries of the Dark Continent are the only ones who truly understand.

Africa is a place that will beckon you to return to it. Your first visit is most often like your first kiss, a wonderful experience, and a playful joyous scamper through paradise, oohing and aahing at the marvels of this foreign world. Chances to taste, smell, see and experience new wonders - the first kiss with Africa makes you fall in love with her. You have to go back for more. Paradise is a big place to discover the first kiss. You are caressed with beautiful vistas and herds of wild game. This enhances and broadens your visions of Mother Nature and the bountiful and beautiful woman she is! It wets your appetite for more. One is like a teenager in love, you thrive to explore her and unlock the secrets of life and death hidden just below her appealing surface. When you dance with this beautiful woman you cannot help but hunger for more even if you know there are places you should not go. One should be wary of the forbidden fruit!

Africa is so sweet and beautiful on her face—so inviting! But the kiss of Africa also reeks of the smell of death. Her warmth and beauty suck you in like a Venus flytrap, inviting you to the life of paradise.

How far do you go? How long do you embrace this woman before it's the last dance! You cannot resist the forbidden fruit tree and the evil and danger that lurk within it. We were meant to be mere mortals, so it is only fate that brings you back to Africa to hunt the most dangerous game on earth!

The face of the bush country of Africa is salted and peppered with critters that will kill you. The danger comes in all shapes and sizes, from the deadly Black Mumba that slithers on the ground to the huge elephants that will stomp you into the dirt if they so desire. There are lions and leopards that can cover 100 yards twelve times faster than the throroughbred horse that will win the Kentucky Derby this year. If these critters are coming at you with fire in their eyes and death in their claws, only seconds separate who will grace this earth shortly!

Cape buffalo will lay and wait to kill an attacker. When they charge, even the biggest guns may not slow them down. In the water, crocodiles, and especially hippos, pose as deadly threats killing hundreds of native folks a year. If that isn't enough there is the rhino - a steel-plated, horned critter with a bad disposition to boot! You think it may be safe after dark in camp, but more than one hyena has tip-toed into camp and clamped onto a human by his skull dragging him from his sleeping bag and disappearing into the darkness. Over the past year (2002) alone, this scenario has played out over sixty times leaving behind only the agonizing cries humans make when they have lost a loved one. We won't even get into the reptiles, bugs and things!

On the first trip to Africa, one is likely to hunt plains game. You can enjoy beautiful vistas of semi-open plateaus scattered with zebra, gazelle, wildebeest and the beautiful and majestic kudu. You stalk an array of wonderful and bizarre antelope, being challenged by their stamina, durability and extremely long shots. In the evening, you return to a luxurious ranch to be pampered by a large staff with fine food and drink. It is love at first sight until you taste the forbidden fruit. Now you become mortal and are susceptible to the consequences of nature and reality. The second time around, your venture takes you deep into the bush where you and your counterparts huddle together in camp at night while predators stalk the dark perimeters.

This time you enjoy the compelling beautiful land called Africa by day but sleep uneasy as the dark side engulfs you at night. If you want to hold this woman's hand before the big alter of the sky, she will test you. She will see if you are worthy. If you cannot stand tall and alone and stare into the mouth of death, then do not think about screwing with Mother Nature.

This is the place where you get to reach inside of yourself and find out what kind of "man" you really are. There are only a few things you can do on this earth to test your mental capacities in the face of death while considering it a recreational activity; perhaps hang gliding off a mountain top, free-boarding down an uncharted snow-capped mountain or free-hand climbing a vertical rock cliff; the latter of which my wife and I did as we climbed to 12,000 feet to hunt Himalayan thar.

The INNER FORCE

In any of these activities, human error can prove disabling or fatal. None of these activities, however, pit you against a living, thinking creature that when pressed, will try to outwit and outmaneuver you in order to kill you. Hunting the dangerous game of Africa is serious business. It is a business where if you hesitate, error, or if your gun misfires, you very well may pay with your life. If you have the honor of still gracing this planet, then perhaps luck or self-preservation is one of your attributes. Then, if your body

Frank Schmitz

is still intact, you will have great memories and stories for your latter years. Such is the thrill of the Dark Continent.

My return to Africa is a trip to hunt Cape buffalo and leopard. If opportunity presents itself, the magnificent sable and the nasty crocodile also could make my hit list. If I see a trophy kudu, the most magnificent antelope of all, my trigger finger surely will become weak. I also have a suicidal craving to do night hunting for other predators - carcan and hyena or whatever the darkness brings forth! This is my allergic reaction to the forbidden fruit of Africa. This is what compels me to do the tango with Miss Africa, a place that abounds with treasure and beauty. A place where the light side is the dark side and life and death is as common as day and night. A place where life is death and death is life, A place where to flee or stand is to live or die - in no particular order.

This country demands you to think outside the "box", to forgo conventional wisdom and rely on instincts to survive or transcend to the eternal life of the next world. This land does not separate from man or beast.

When you dance with Mother Nature, you had better hold onto her hand tightly because as she so gracefully floats and spins, she discards the weak, sick and feeble-minded until only the strongest and wisest remain. She does not care if you can talk the talk. You better be able to walk the walk or this is the last dance for you!

My destination in Africa is Zimbabwe, the wildest and most beautiful country of all and home of perhaps the greatest wonder of the earth - Victoria Falls. This country provides a wide range of habitat that is conducive to free ranging herds of many species of animals including the big five - elephant, rhino, leopard, lion and Cape buffalo. as well as all aforementioned dangerous game.

This beautiful country itself is a reflection of the forbidden fruit for it is in turmoil. and uprising. With government support, native people have overthrown and killed some white folks. The world community has warned that the country is unstable and to be on guard while there. Hopefully we will see none of that.

My Journey Begins

Yesterday I left my teary-eyed wife, Terri, waving good-bye to me in the Lewiston, Idaho airport to begin the hideous three days of travel to Zimbabwe. Human harassment started early with a one-hour fifteen minute delay at Seattle, Washington, while agents tore apart my gear. I did eventually get through with my guns and ammo. Sixty rounds of ammo had earlier been confiscated in Chicago, Illinois, when my brother, Tim, tried to deliver my favorite rounds to me on an Idaho bear hunt. I guess it is the price we pay for Nine-Eleven (9/11/2001); it seems the terrorism continues!

Today I travel from Seattle, Washington; to Dallas, Texas; to London, England; to Harare, Africa. This tour started at 6:00 a.m. in Seattle and will end the next day at 10:00 p.m. in Harare - some forty hours later. My ass should conform to the shape of an airplane seat by then. With the time change from home to Zimbabwe, I will be hunting on a fourteen-hour time difference that will always be tomorrow. I could call home and say, "Hey, guess what I shot tomorrow—a sable!"

I am a licensed guide and outfitter in Idaho and always preach, "know your gun and how to shoot it." Well, I borrowed a gun for this hunt. It is a 375 H&H, but it is a Browning A-bolt model. I am very familiar with it seeing as I have three others. I also brought my trusty 7mm Mag (A-bolt), which has been to and killed in Africa before. I call my 7mm Mag the ultimate killing machine (U.K.M). It has put down over forty big game animals from many regions of the earth. My favorite bullet, the 160-grain nosler partition has previously killed grizzly, moose, eland, kudu, elk and thar, always performing exceptionally well. This was the type of ammo donated to the men in blue in Chicago.

On this hunt, I will use 160-grain weatherby spears instead. They seem to shoot as well. I hope they can do the job at crunch time. The 375 H&H, I have named "Dick" seeing as his owner, Dave Futh, has a similar but more graphic nickname. I will shoot 300-grain solids with "Dick." When shooting a 375 at dangerous game at close range, it doesn't matter if you can split a gnat's hair at 300 yards. What matters is if you can knock the air out of one of those critters before he makes you say "uncle." A charging Cape buffalo has a bad habit of not only wanting to run over you like a freight train but he also likes to "hook" you. The hook happens at the time you think you are going to be spread down the tracks for a quarter of a mile. He tips his head imbedding his curved horn into your belly button and effortlessly tosses you over his head, disemboweling you on the way. Then he spreads you down the railroad tracks for a quarter mile. So, you see if a mad buffalo is charging you — you do not want a bullet that will just put a hole in his roof. You want to cave the whole fricking roof and attic in — right now!

If you shoot at a charging leopard, the effect you want to see is the needle to a balloon effect, the big bang and total deflation. A charging leopard is like a Tasmanian devil; a wild, fast, spinning ball of fur - except the leopard has claws and fangs hanging out of it. If this fur ball spins into you before total deflation, its jaws will clamp onto your head while its claws continue to spin, decorating the brush around you with your guts like ornaments on a Christmas tree. So, hopefully I will shoot fast and straight if crunch time comes my way. If "Dick" does his job, the critter will be screwed. If "Dick" does not, I may be the one taking the screwing. I think I have selected my hunting partners well, with "Dick" (375) and U.K.M (7mm).

My last trip to the "Holy Land" of Africa, U.K.M. put on a performance of a lifetime, making me look like a hired gun. It dropped the tiny val rhebok at 400 yards, a warthog at 350 yards on the run, and two Cape kudu both on the run at 450 yards and 600 yards. The latter being the shot of a lifetime—off hand across a mountain. I doubt if I ever can score a perfect ten on the balancing beams again. Surely my aerobatic ability has subsided.

A new segment of my journey has begun. I have heard horror stories of transfers through Great Britain. The Brits act like they are America's greatest allies, but they only kiss our butt so we protect them. Without us, the world would squash those lazy infidels instantly. The Brits hate hunting and especially hate the American John Wayne attitude. When you come to Britain, they know how to roll out the red carpet for you. First they confiscated my checked-through luggage. Then they forced me to go through British Customs as if I was coming to England to reclaim my luggage. There they explained how they do not allow guns into their country and I would need an import permit from their government instead of Zimbabwe. Besides that, they have

The INNER FORCE

an embargo against Zimbabwe because they have had a civil war for the last year. (News to the rest of the third world countries like the U.S.A.) They gave me the friendly drop your pants body search and pat down and then confiscated both my guns!! The blasted bloody wieners!

I was released thirty minutes prior to take-off. A customs agent asked me if I wanted to call either of their two buddies to arrange to get my guns through the country. It would require paying his contact to arrange my flights through some other countries and I would be detained until it is done; that my friend is called blackmail in the rest of the less civilized world.

The customs agents said, "We can straighten this matter out in a day or two and get you on your way!"

I told them from the third world country I am from, there is a saying for matters such as this my friend, "f-ck you." I then proceeded to the gate where I got another courteous pat down and my carry-on bag was confiscated! This may ruin all twelve rolls of film I have when it goes through the x-ray machine. Also it is now twenty minutes before departure, so I do not know if my carry-on bag with my camera and the only change of clothes is on my flight. I also remembered as I boarded the Harare flight to Zimbabwe that my traveler checks and cash were in my carry-on bag, too. It will be another eleven hours before I know if I have any luggage in Zimbabwe. If not, I am wearing a dress shirt and pants with cowboy boots. I have no guns and maybe a camera with ruined film. Thanks, Great Britain. I hope Ireland storms your castle and performs sodomy with Prince Charles to up-breed your in-breeds. I realize this treatment at the time does not portray all the fine common citizens of Great Britain. I can imagine that many a Brits have had negative experiences on the shores of the U.S.A. So to all the good folks, I apologize for my critical thoughts.

At least if there is a civil war going on in Zimbabwe, there should be plenty of guns around, probably all old SKS's. I'll be the first to try and kill dangerous game with a 7.59 round. Maybe I will opt for spear-chucking or snaring—traditional methods of the impoverished native folks.

Somehow I am in Harare and it is Thursday night. It never really got dark last night as we flew into the sun. The city is third world, but the Meikles Hotel is as modern as any I have ever been in.

Frank Schmitz

It was intimidating in the Harare Airport seeing as there were hundreds of people there, but only one fair skinned one, "MonWha." I expected someone from the outfitting camp to greet me, but was left to fend for myself. I thought the Meikles Hotel would have an airport pickup, but found out it did not. I then realized that I would have to hire a taxicab. I narrowly averted another major disaster when I put my folder with this journal, passport and airline tickets on a cart that I loaded with my other luggage (that I was happy to see had arrived). My folder had been five-fingered. We loaded my luggage in the taxi and drove twenty minutes to the hotel before I realized it was missing. My taxi driver, Fungue, and I raced back to the airport, but the folder was gone and surprise nobody knew anything!

I offered a reward for its return and there was more discussion. The reward I offered was one hundred US dollars. That is big time money in this part of the world but peanuts compared to not recovery my folder. It was reported that they had seen it recovered by a certain individual. He was located. Upon some inquiry it was reported to have been turned in. After another drawn out search and additional discussion, the folder and its contents were returned to me. All was there, except my good pen. It was obvious that the folder had been probed, but I was relieved to have my passport, cities permits, visa and export permits back. So, I would not have to become a Zimbabwe citizen! Back at the luxurious Meikles Hotel, I have not been able to fax or e-mail any information about my missing guns to the U.S. The business office opens in the morning at 7:30 when the U.S. is asleep. I believe it would be 10:30 p.m. the day before at that time. So I still am not able to contact anyone.

I have been propositioned by two women of the night so far which equates to a one per hour average. Naturally they are black women and are stunningly beautiful. The oldest business on earth is alive and well in Zimbabwe. AIDS also ravages Zimbabwe, although I think that it is confined mainly to the uneducated population in the country. The city folks look extremely healthy. They are kind, courteous and very helpful. Of course, they all crave the American dollar and would be willing to do anything to get some green backs.

I was really pissed at the damn Brits for swiping my guns, but my booking agent obviously screwed up big time by not knowing about these problems. Blair Worldwide is a reputable booking

The INNER FORCE

agent, but this was a huge oversight on their part. So much for practicing and being familiar with your weapons before hunting the most dangerous game on earth. I am confident that I will come up with a gun of some kind. Fortunately, I was able to confuse the simple-minded Brit custom agent and switch my ammo back into my baggage. I was concerned they would spot it in the x-ray machine and confiscate all my other gear, but luckily it came through. So maybe I can find a 375 or 7 Mag of some sort to shoot the ammo.

As I tried to sleep last night at the hotel, I wondered what lies ahead for me on this adventure. Not only am I not sure who I will hunt with but I wonder what will I hunt with.

Nothing enhances your ability afield more than familiar equipment. These are your tools and the saying: "You are only as good as your tools" goes a long way toward describing my aprehension.

I have been fortunate enough to have hunted many species in many places. I have used shotguns, muzzleloaders, bows and rifles. I have witnessed some surprisingly quick kills administered by three razor blades on a fletched aluminum shaft. I have seen 225 grain bullets delivered by a gun called a 338 not do the job!

The situation that comes to mind is a snow-covered mountainside in British Columbia. I am laying between our decoys (our horses) as a herd of mountain caribou approach us. A good bull reluctantly follows his harem into the trap. Two double lung shots do not put this animal on the ground. Although dead on his feet he struggles ahead towards his harem. Wanting to end the suffering I double lung him a third time- this time knocking his front legs out from under him, causing his white muzzle to crash to the ground. Yet his back legs still stand, this from an animal not known for being shock resistant. Then, still unwilling to leave this earth and his harem of girls, this caribou gallantly lifts his head and pushes with his front legs until unbelievably he stands once again. I don't know if the fourth shot finally did him in or if he just ran out of blood, but it destroyed my confidence in my 338. Later while packing my pet gun, my trusty 7-mag (now in royal storage in England) shooting 160 grain bullets, I easily and cleanly killed a 60-inch moose and a grizzly bear.

African game has a reputation for being tough to kill. The native folks will tell you that you must not only kill their first

Frank Schmitz

spirit, but also their second spirit. I have seen some of them take a tremendous pounding before relinquishing their second spirit.

The dainty little springbuck most graciously relinquishes its second spirit. After it is dead on the ground, suddenly the hair along its back will stand up and emit a very pleasant lavender type of fragrance. When my springbuck did this my tracker commented "second spirit leave now." Moments later the hair relaxed back down but then the scenario reoccurred. The surprised tracker commented, " He have third spirit."

Well I doubt many folks believe in black magic or numerous spirits. I can say I have witnessed my share of strange things but an incident occurred in Africa that defies reality the last time I graced this soil.

I shot a beast of remarkable beauty called a gemsbok. They are tan on their backs with a spectacular marked black and white face. Gracing their heads are two long straight black horns of 30 inches or so. They are stout, weighing in at about 500 pounds. I shot one as he trotted past my hiding place (as I was tucked under an appropriately named Ame bush while waiting in ambush) taking four double lung shots. As I ran up to him he sat like a dog and looked like a pincushion. I could hear him breathing through the entrance and exit wounds as I delivered a "coupe de grace" to the handsome beast.

The INNER FORCE

But that stamina paled in comparison to the endurance of a blue wildebeest I hunted. We had come across this particular bull early one morning. As he fled I poured three rounds into him until he disappeared into dense underbrush. We waited an hour for him to stiffen up and die before following him into the bush. After another hour and a half stalk, suddenly he stood before me in the dry African savanna. I shot him in the front shoulder as he turned trying to take off. He ran in a tight circle and I shot him again. He started to spin like a Tasmanian devil with a huge cloud of dust enveloping him. My P.H. (professional hunter) said he is done, as the ornery beast disappeared in his self-inflicted whirlwind of dust.

My guide congratulated me as the cloud of dust slowly drifted off. We looked in disbelief as I asked, "Where is the wildebeest?"

We stared into the bush thinking our eyes defied us, but the burly critter was gone!

Not to worry my P.H. informed me. We are within two hundred yards of the corner of this fenced area. That wildebeest is in no shape to jump a fence so we will spread out forming a triangle and walk to the inside corner, thus forcing him into a corner. Sounded good, so we quickly organized this drive of sorts and converged into the corner. No wildebeest!

After a quick search there was a spec of blood across the four-strand fence. He had cleared it. We followed the surprisingly scant blood trail for several hundred yards until we could look into a valley in front of us. The landscape that unfolded in front of me was a huge valley, with open plain that stretched out as far as the eye could see. An endless wild chunk of Africa, but surely he could not have gone far. Once again we spread out and began to comb the valley. Nothing. We searched in a grid fashion. Surely he was dead and it was just a matter of time until we would stumble across him. This search continued for the beast from morning into the afternoon. As the sun sank towards the western horizon the reality of defeat sank in. We gathered up and all climbed into a land rover. I got in the open back with the trackers forgoing the place of honor - the front seat. I now had my 338 in hand when an excited tracker blurted the only English he knew, "Buffalo". Pointing to a high ridge above us. Low and behold there was the wildebeest. He had never gone into the valley below, but instead ran in a hook type pattern to the top of the ridge. There he sat all day watching us search below him. As the truck ground to a stop, the wildebeest sensed he had been spotted. Again he rose to his feet and absorbed two additional shots from my 338. The weak beast collapsed to the ground as we rejoiced. I ran to him wondering where I had hit him and how often I had missed since he endured so long. When I arrived where the dead beast now lay, to my amassment seven shots had entered this beast. Five went into his front shoulders and upper chest while two tore threw his neck. All appeared to be good killing shots. I was beside myself as I examined this resilient critter and commented that he must have had a lot more than a second spirit. Then as if to acknowledge that comment in a scene fit for a Hollywood horror story. The dead beast came back to life! He lifted his head and made a wide-eyed gasp, then collapsed to the ground, still dead or then dead. I don't know which! What I do know is I have witnesses, but furthermore, I was video taping this entire episode. The tape is intact - video and audio. It will make you wonder about black magic, witchcraft, the second spirit and the after life.

It is Friday and my air travel is complete. I will go for coffee and see if I can make any communication to the outside world. Hopefully a representative of Shangani Safaris will show up or maybe Lloyd Yateman, the P.H. and we can resolve my dilemmas.

The exchange rate here is 75 - 80 Zim dollars to a U.S. dollar, so something that costs $300, is really $4 U.S. The natives will rip you off in a heartbeat, but on the other hand they want U.S. money bad enough that I had one fellow offer me 400 Zim for $1 U.S, which is a significant difference in buying power.

I saw a tanned zebra hide in the open market place this morning that was $140,000 Zim. At 75 to 1, that is $2,000 U.S. and too much money. But at 400 to 1, it is $350 U.S. and a very good deal. So if bartering is in place here, I will work towards a 400 to 1 exchange for good buys.

Jet lag seems to be taking a toll on me today as I am trying to function at mid-morning (10:30 a.m.), when it is 1:30 a.m. at home. I think I'll be adjusted after another day. Seeing as I only slept six hours in the past three days, I will sleep well tonight and probably shock myself into Africa time.

My attempts to communicate to the outside failed and the people at the front desk seemed to be unaware of Shangani Safaris. I wondered if I was going anywhere from here. Fungue my taxi cab driver stopped by at mid-morning to see if I needed his services. He wants to take me to the country side to hunt. It turns out he has never seen any wild game of Africa before but has only heard stories of them. He also has no idea how to secure a firearm. I tell him to check and see if I am still here tomorrow.

About noon, to my relief, my agent picked me up to take me to our hunting area Chiredzi. We will hunt southeast Zimbabwe along the Gonarcahou National Park. The six-hour drive proved quite interesting. The distance from Harare to Chiredzi is 418 miles. The road is black topped. I got to see lots of the twelve million people in Zimbabwe. The road is used as a trail, so there is a continuous line of people on the road. The cars drive 80 mph (140 km) and are buzzing in and around folks at high speed. The fact that we did not kill 100 people on the way there amazed me!

My driver was particularly proud of having a driver's license. To have a drivers license elevates a person from the lower class, making them a middle class person, a person of status. He took it to heart that he was a professional driver and the envy of the majority of native folks.

The people of Zimbabwe are very proud and dress exceptionally well. In the city the women wear nice dresses and the men all have dress pants and shirts, often with ties or uniforms. They are easily better dressed than Americans in the U.S. In the countryside, their attire is more tattered and worn as the standard of living falls off remarkably from the city. Here the folks live in masonry circular huts with thatched roofs and dirt floors. The huts are constructed of baked clay blocks and stucco. The average house is about a sixteen-foot circle.

Frank Schmitz

    They have no windows and some have no doors, just open frames. I am sure there is little to nothing inside them, as the inhabitants eke out a living on the land, surviving on what crops they can grow or animals they raise. As we traveled through the open savanna and entered thicker bush country, the hut construction changed to logs with stucco. Of the thousands of people I have been seeing since leaving the city, I have not seen a single white person.

    The unfortunate side of this ride was realizing that Zimbabwe is developing faster than one thinks. The countryside within 350 miles of Harare is fenced with livestock being tended to. There are plantations of corn, wheat, sugar cane and tobacco. Wildlife has been exterminated in this area, even though the people own no weapons. They have managed to capture every last springbok and other animals (including the predators) with wire snares. Only funding from hunting and trophy fees will save what is left. Seeing this made me appreciate how vast and untamed Idaho still is. The wild areas that are left in Zimbabwe surround the national parks

The INNER FORCE

and these refuges have saved the indigenous animals. Poaching is a big problem. In the parks they shoot to kill the poachers! This approach has lessened the poachers. Luckily, Zimbabwe is blessed with many sizeable parks.

Near dark we arrived at a luxurious base camp. The huts here have stone floors, stone walls, and thatched roofs. The camp is set alongside a river where I could hear codfish and crocodiles splashing around in the darkness. My P.H. is named Nixon. He is very well educated and a fluent in English. My tracker and skinner are natives also. I cannot remember their names, but I think I will call them Gravedigger and Bones, defining the reality of their jobs. Nixon has a 375 H&H for me to use and was glad to hear I was able to retrieve my ammo. Ammo is in very short supply and hard to come by. It currently is not being sold or brought into Zimbabwe. I was surprised to find out I am the only honky in camp, as well as the only hunter. The owner, his sons, and families have apparently fled the country and are now scattered about in England and New Zealand. They left four months ago, which happens to be the same time they were assuring me all was well in Zimbabwe. He even said, "Do you think I would leave my wife and kids there if I thought there was danger at all?" Apparently, Pinocchio, I mean Lloyd has a pretty long nose.

The natives kept telling me he was on business in Harare and perhaps he was. If so, why didn't he greet me at the airport? That is his business. I never did meet Lloyd during the duration of this hunt, so I can only speculate that he was not around. I did meet some of his family and relatives. Some where in the process of selling and moving, others had gone overseas, perhaps temporarily, while yet others were determined to stay at home. Some did not have the financial resources to leave and at least one women involved in the operation was staying at her place in town. This explains why I did not see one white person in the entire countryside. White people seem to be as scarce and endangered as the wild game around Harare. The good news is Nixon has had four hunters before me without incident, plus he is letting me use his gun!

Speaking of white people in danger, I heard at camp that Mark Sullivan from Tanzania finished playing his game of chess. Sullivan has produced many videos on lion, leopard and Cape buffalo hunting. Mark Sullivan and his producers always try to initiate charges for good video. After watching one of his last releases, I told my brother Tim that he was going to kill one of his clients by playing games with Cape buffalo. Well, rumor has it that on the last tape he filmed a lion kills him while they are walking up to the lion showing their last respects. I hope it was worth the fame and glory because Mark has some sweet, young children who must miss him dearly. (After I returned home to investigate the story, I found that it was only a rumor and to my knowledge he is not injured but instead carries on. His brave exploits leave his competitors in envy probably hoping for an ill-fated incident.)

As a matter of fact trying to write a book is a rather long and sometimes painful experience. So a year and a half passed between my initial writing and re-writing and finding a publisher. In that time I spoke to Mark at S.C.I National Convention who is undoubtedly alive and well. We joked of his ill-fated departure from earth and I would sure be honored to hunt with this man some day.

Tomorrow the hunt begins. I have made it clear that leopard is the main trophy for me, so Nixon is going to set twelve baits in the morning. He said we would not fool around and get to business on that. I have a feeling this will be a most interesting hunt!

I had just put this journal down and went to relieve myself when a six-inch lizard ran over my foot. Now it is hiding under my bed. It is probably a good thing my wife, Terri, could not come along on this hunt!

I lay awake, trying to sleep, but instead wonder what lies ahead, I wonder what Terri is doing and reflect upon past hunting adventures. I cannot help but ponder if there will be close encounters on this adventure and what they might be. Close encounters come in many forms! Part of what makes hunting so exciting is the adrenaline rush we get when we finally come face to face with the wild game we pursue, or the challenges that nature brings forth.

The thrill of the hunt! That's what makes hunters lie awake at night, in anticipation to see if we can outwit the game we pursue. Often it leads to what is commonly known as "buck fever." The long awaited opportunity finally presents itself and suddenly we feel unprepared and unable to react. Our legs and arms turn to rubber and we find ourselves incapable of utilizing the weapon at hand - rifle, bow, or whatever . Many times I have bugled in a rutting bull only to have the hunter melt down and become incapable of drawing his bow, or not even thinking of shooting as he is in awe of the majestic beast. Their reactions vary from pure frustration to "Holy cow did you see that?" Many a trophy whitetail or elk hunter went home with memories of failure that left the hunter happy for the experience or in pure frustration for blowing the chance of a lifetime . Everybody reacts to these encounters differently. But then there are other types of close confrontations, too. Ones that literally are heart stopping. Ones that put your life in eminent danger! These encounters are deeply embedded in your mind and will either drive you on or make you realize that you have traveled too far out of your element. Speaking for myself, I had several close encounters with wild game that gave me tremendous adrenaline rushes. I cherish these moments that separate the sameness of normal life from the intense reality of the hunt.

   I was blessed to marry a woman that shares my obsession for adventure, and adventure she has had!

   Terri is not only a wonderful cook in our hunting camps, she routinely does pack-ins and tends to duties normally associated with tough male figures. All this from a petite lady, all five feet and a hundred pounds of her. She has made some of the best shots I have ever seen. She shot her first whitetail buck at a full run at several hundred yards, just as it was clearing a barbwire fence. She hit it in full flight as it sailed over the fence only to land graveyard dead on the other side. Another time while fishing with women companions off of the shores of Kodiak Island, her captain spotted a trophy black tail buck high upon a rocky embankment. Knowing that she had a deer tag and rifle he instructed her to take aim. As the boat rocked in three-foot swells, he told her to stand free without a rest and let her rifle sights sway back and forth past the buck until she thought the time was right. With a single shot she dropped the buck where it stood. That's my lady!

   Getting back to close encounters, Terri has always had a passion for bear hunting. Why I do not know!

Frank Schmitz

One time while hunting with our notorious guide (and equally as good a storyteller as myself), Chuck Pollencheck from northern Wisconsin, he took her to a bear bait that I had previously hunted. A tree stand had been built between a pair of poplars that stood near the bait. The stand was constructed of 2x4's and plywood with 2x4 steps ascending to the platform. The morning before I had left a foamy pad wedged between the two trees that I sat in. Upon arriving in the afternoon we found the foamy pad had blown to the ground the night before. It had been shredded to pieces by incoming bears. As I assisted Terri up the tree to the perch of the evening hunt, I noticed claw marks – yes from a bear that

The INNER FORCE

had climbed into the stand the night before. Obviously it, not the wind had pulled the piece of foam rubber out before tearing it to shreds. It is not comforting to know a bear was residing in your tree stand! Being the gamer she is, she took that stand and later harvested her first black bear.

Another time we had placed a tree stand on an active bait where Terri was to observe and videotape bear activity for other clients. Upon setting the stand up I placed a rock on the platform telling her that if she needed to chase a bear away she could throw the rock at him to spook him off. Loyally she took the stand that night, camera in hand and waited. Nothing came in as darkness overtook the forest. Using a rope she lowered the camera to the ground. As Terri started to descend the tree she looked around. Seemingly out of nowhere, there stood a sow with a cub! Quickly Terri climbed back into her stand hoping they would leave shortly. The bear persisted so she whistled and yelled at them. The old sow ignored this interruption so she proceeded with the first line of defense, hurling the rock at a nearby tree. Ignoring the rock the bear gorged themselves on Ripon Good Cookies. Finally, as darkness encompassed the forest they moved off into the brush. Terri quickly climbed down and ran for her life to a nearby logging road where she met Chuck's wife, Sharon, waiting in a pick up truck. Sharon had figured all was not right, but she was damned if she was going to walk into the woods unarmed, knowing that Terri was probably treed.

In latter years with a couple bears under her belt, Terri became obsessed with wanting to harvest a brown colored-phased black bear. Terri had taken bear in Wisconsin and in Idaho with Darrel Weddle, but the color of cinnamon, brown or blond had eluded her.

I had bought a bear hunt at an auction at the SCI fundraiser in Saskatchewan with John Woulfe. The first go around Terri shot herself yet another black- black bear. We rebooked with John and the next spring found ourselves back in their good company. On this hunt Terri would see the color-phased bear of her dreams. Unfortunately the big chocolate bruin turned out to be a sow with three cubs - two brown and one black. She enjoyed the Disneyland camaraderie of watching the cubs frolic around with mama at the bait. The cubs would chase each other back and forth occasionally running into each other and falling over. While they were romping and rolling around they suddenly disappeared below her tree.

Frank Schmitz

    The comical amusement of watching these siblings turned quite hair raising as she heard them ascend the very tree she sat in. Terri remained motionless, almost afraid to breath as they scampered up the base of the tree. Soon one of the cubs was directly behind her head making soft peeping sounds. The cub investigated this foreign tree squirrel, letting mom know the whole time that something strange was in this tree. As Terri sat still , frozen in terror, the cub began to pull at her long wavy locks of hair. She thought, "Oh My God," if the mother bear looks up to inspect her beloved little cubs and sees me, "There will be hell to pay!" The thought of shooting the mother in self-defense and orphaning the helpless cubs was indeed unpleasant and an unacceptable predicament. On the other hand being mauled by any angry mother bear was not an option.

The INNER FORCE

Frank Schmitz

    The notion raced through her mind, "Do I have enough time to make a warning shot to avert an attack? If unsuccessful, do I still have time to shoot again?" At that moment "mama" directed her attention to her cubs and the frozen silhouette in the tree, sensing something was not right she let out a soft woof. As she approached the tree and disappeared out of sight below her, Terri's emotions were running rampant . Two of the cubs saw mom coming and headed down the tree towards her. The third cub, still curious as to what he found in the tree, was busy with his investigation. Mom appeared again sending another warning to him and down the tree he went to join his siblings. They vanished as quickly as they had come, leaving a rattled and relived hunter in a tree. That clarifies the meaning of "A hair raising experience." To date Terri has missed one good colored-phased bear since then, but will inevitably succeed. That's hunting!

    A close encounter of a different kind happened to a friend of mine while we hunted above the Artic Circle. Duke Potter, Tom Jacobs, and I went on an adventure to the top of the world to hunt musk ox. Our common bond is that we are all self-made entrepreneurs - guys who had forgone college and instead built our business through blood, sweat, tears, common sense and a lot of hard work. We had heard horror stories of hunters battling the extreme elements, snow, wind and bitter cold. Temperatures 60 to 80 degrees below zero and chill factors that would freeze exposed flesh in seconds. Equipment that was despicable and undependable. We figured that we could avoid these perils by taking advantage of an unusual opportunity to hunt in August - before the winter freeze sets in. Little did we know that the Eskimo's summer equipment was probably in worse shape then their winter gear. As we prepared for this artic adventure we underestimated the elements of danger that lie ahead. A brush with fate was forth coming for one of us, but if you are willing to roll the dice you have to be willing to accept the consequences of "Snake Eyes."

    Our adventure began on the shore of the artic ocean at the mouth of Ellice River where our soon to be Eskimo friends met our plane that had just landed on the beach. The Eskimos had a half dozen old 14-foot aluminum boats powered by 5 and 7 horse Evinrude motors. They intended to gather up our gear and provisions and transport us on the river seven miles inland to camp. The camp was a small Eskimo tent village that included women and children. They were gathering fish and air-drying them for winter consumption. There were caribou shoulders scattered on the beach, some partially consumed while others waited to be carved upon. These people live simple as simple can be, utilizing the land to sustain themselves. We stayed in a small 8x8 plywood shack with two windows, a door, two wooden bunks and a cook stove. This would be home for a week. The country was vast with open rolling hills, hundreds of miles above timberline. Scattered herds of caribou dotted the land in the distant horizon.

The first morning I glassed over a hundred and seventy caribou at one time. None were within a mile of camp. I'm sure we could see seven miles and beyond with not one musk ox in sight. That morning we motored up and down stream to parts unknown. The technology for how far to go was simple, take a spare full gas can with you. You go one way until you run out of gas. Then fill your gas tank with the spare gas and return back to camp. Should make it! Unless you had a tail wind going out and a head wind coming in, then it was bye bye for you.

Another uncomfortable fact was that the boats leaked - badly! When we would push off of shore to go, I would start bailing water with a coffee can. Once we got going, you would simply pull the plug in the back of the boat and let the forward momentum of the boat suck the water out the back. We always had a constant water flow - not a good thing if you run out of gas.

Oh well, at least I wont have to put up with the Artic winter like my friend Lad Shunnenson had to. When he went hunting it was so cold they buried him under caribou hides in a sled that was pulled behind a snowmobile driven by a hardy Eskimo. Lying in the sled buried in hides he never knew when they would be going over heaved ice chunks. The unsuspecting and jarring bumps of the sled bouncing over jagged ice ended up breaking both his elbows. Worse yet, another fellow was in a sled when the Eskimo jumped a ledge, ejecting him out onto the ice. There he lay as the sleds raced out of sight, not realizing they had lost their client. The temperature was so cold that life expectancy without warm hides or fire was estimated at 25 minutes. Fortunately the natives realized their cargo was gone and retrieved him in time. How the thick-skinned natives survive is a mystery to the rest of the world.

Frank Schmitz

The first day the musk ox eluded all of us, but I did harvest a good caribou that had a 50 plus inch spread. My guide, "The Fonz," and I stalked him for several hours, but the bull always kept his distance at 450-500 yards. Finally, I informed The Fonz that I thought I could shoot him at 450 yards. He argued, "No too far, too far Frank- him to far." Laying on the ground with my gun resting on my backpack, I zeroed my trusty companion in. When my old tattered 7 mag spoke the caribou crumpled in his tracks, graveyard dead. The Fonz grabbed my spent cartridge and said, "That very good shot, this my trophy," as he held up the casing.

Towards evening we gathered back at camp for a caribou steak dinner. Lady luck had only shown on me. We exchanged stories while entertaining a small gathering of Eskimo children. It was getting closer to sunset, which occurs at 11:30 PM this time of the year, when one of the teenage boys came running and yelling, "Muck Ox." There across the river on the horizon stood a lone bull. Big old bulls that are no longer strong enough to maintain herd dominancy are pushed from the herd by a younger bull and abandoned. They aimlessly wonder around until a predator - wolf or human dispatches them. Duke drew the lucky straw to have at him and he did.

They crossed the river stalking up towards the musk ox, hidden by the eroded riverbank, as we watched from across the way. Soon a shot rang out and the musk ox's hindquarters dropped to the ground. Half down and half to go as the next shot killed the front half. The celebration was on as we recovered Duke's fine trophy.

Musk ox is an animal similar to a buffalo except they have tremendously long, thick shaggy coats of hair that drape to the ground. They look prehistoric and kind of silly yet are big enough to be a little intimidating when you get close to them. They charge occasionally, usually as a bluff, but it's enough to make you respect them. We would learn afterwards that Duke's musk ox would make number 32 all time in Boone and Crockett's record book. Awesome! Later in the hunt Duke would bag a caribou that would outscore Tom's and mine and narrowly miss the record book also. That is Duke! A great competitor and the most organized man I have ever been associated with. Duke is always prepared and never over looks a detail.

Several days passed before the ocean laid down enough for our small crafts to venture out on it. Today is the day to head to sea. Twenty-some miles out lies an island that is about seven

The INNER FORCE

miles wide and twenty-four miles long. On it is a herd of about 40stranded musk ox waiting for the Artic Ocean to turn back to ice. In the winter they wander aimlessly, unable to distinguish land from sea. The frozen snow covered ocean looks the same as the frozen snow covered land to them. They paw through the snow looking for lichen moss to feed on, invariably ending up on an island or main land where they linger until the next season. If the ice breaks up while on the island, that is where they stay. The Eskimos knew that they would be there, so they took Tom out across the ocean to the island.

The Fonz and I headed east up the mainland shore in search of the shaggy beast. We stopped periodically and climbed upon a knob, and glassing inland for a while before moving on. It was perhaps the fourth or fifth stop while glassing from a vantage point, I spotted an aluminum boat washed up on the shore. it was three quarters of a mile off to the west, capsized and rising in and out of the tide. Upon reporting the sighting to The Fonz he responded, " Where, me no see boat?" I pointed out the direction and traded my 20x80 powered binoculars for his tattered 8x Tascos. One side of his bino's was knocked out so he used them as monoculars, holding them sideways, peeking through the one good side. He peered through my big glasses and soon said, "Oh me find new boat" Without giving any thought or consideration to what had happened to the fellows whom had been lost in that boat, we gathered up our gear to go investigate the new find. Upon close inspection we found the new boat had even more holes in it then the one we were using. It was pretty battered up from rising in and out of the rocky shoreline. The fateless crew apparently fed crab on the ocean floor.

A couple more stops up the beach and our motor sputtered to a halt, out of gas. We refilled the tank with our spare can and started home. Where the Ellice River poured into the sea there was a series of sandbars and rock out-croppings, many protruding above the water line. These randomly scattered little rock islands extended out into the ocean for perhaps a mile. We had to be careful not to beach ourselves in the falling tide when entering the main riverbed. I was daydreaming of musk ox when we nearly bottomed out. The Fonz quickly pulled the trusty Evinrude lower unit out of the water to prevent its propeller from being damaged and in doing so choked the motor. We drifted momentarily as I bailed water and the Fonz pulled the starter rope to fire the motor

Frank Schmitz

back up. Just as the motor turned over and the Fonz dropped it back in the water to send us on our way, I heard a rifle shot. It sounded as it if came from the ocean. I asked The Fonz, " Did you hear that?"

"What?" Responded Fonz.

"That shot."

"Ha, Hey me hear it!"

"Well, who would be shooting out in the ocean?" I thought and asked aloud.

"Me no know! Maybe trouble?"

"Stop the motor and let me glass out there!" I ordered, to which he killed the motor.

I started to glass the horizon of this endless plane of water when way out on a rocky ledge I saw some arms frantically waving. "Somebody is out there Fonz!" I exclaimed. We started the motor and headed out into the wide-open blue waters. As we approached I could see a boat marooned against the rocks. It was Tom and his guide. Their engine had blown and they had drifted into the rocks - at sea, stranded, no radio, no nothing! If we had not killed the motor going over that sand bar, we would have headed up river to camp and never have heard his gun shot. Tom and his guide would have been lost at sea for the night to face the rising tide. If the wind had come up that night nobody would have been able to go search for them - perhaps for days. If they weren't washed away by then, hypothermia certainly would have presented a grave danger. These natives don't respect Mother Nature much. But I can tell you Tom was really happy to see me that day. The motor had failed on the return trip. Tom had taken a Musk Ox. So on the bright side of that mishap, he had his musk ox. We towed them in without further incident.

On the second to last day I got my musk ox. Ironically, not only did all of our musk ox make Boone and Crockett record book but also they all placed in the top 100....an extremely rare feat. Mine, to Dukes dismay, edged out his on the B+C score as well as shattering the then world record for Safari Club International. (I never entered it in either book.)

The hunt was remarkably successful yet the lack of respect for Mother Nature coupled with poor equipment was a recipe for disaster...disaster we were lucky to avoid.

Back in Africa I have slept for five hours and now lay awake for an hour listening to the night creatures talking in the bush. My windows are made of screen so no sound is muffled. I hear a monkey and the water splash as a croc's teeth lock shut on some critter that has ventured too close to the shore for a drink. The country is in a severe drought and many people could starve by spring. You would not know it by looking at them. It is not like the commercials we see on T.V. As a matter of fact, everything here is different than what is told to the outside world.

Frank Schmitz

The INNER FORCE

People of Zimbabwe

These people are honest and proud. They do not care about material things. They only want dignity, respect and freedom. It has become vividly clear to me why the Brits took my guns and searched me like a damned terrorist. I thought they were crazy when they said there is a civil war going on in Zimbabwe, but it is true. Zimbabwe, like most African nations, was a British colony under white rule.

Frank Schmitz

The blacks have been enslaved for centuries. Several hundred years ago big wooden boats floated the high seas filled with chained, shackled, and locked slaves on the way to America. The truth is they were sold to white slave traders by their own people. Back then the first black tribes to get weapons from the Europeans quickly conquered and sold the tribesmen of their neighboring tribes. It was the same in America. The first Indian tribes to attain guns from mountain men for furs quickly attacked and decimated other Indian nations. The development of the Americas and Africa are mirror images, for soon after the Indian nations and black tribes scattered their enemies, whites moved in with superior power and force defeating them and laying claim to all the land. The blacks in Africa have been enslaved ever since.

In the 1960s, when human rights came to a head in America, the whites in control of Africa should have been paying closer attention. History always repeats itself, but "man" in all his divine wisdom is a slow learner, not gaining much knowledgefrom his past. Here in Africa, the people are uniting—they have a dream! Just as Martin Luther King in his famous "I Have a Dream" speech declared, "We hold these truths to be self-evident that all men are created equal." That is what the black people of Africa want—Freedom and Equality. The same thing we wanted, fought for and received.

Yes, there is a civil war going on in Zimbabwe; a country that has been controlled by British rule and British descendents. Yes, blacks have risen up, killing and taking land from white owners; an evolutionary process that was inevitable. The people are becoming educated and realize that the ideas they have are right and true. The United Kingdom listens to their people whom are losing control and fleeing the country. Great Britain has imposed an embargo and other sanctions against Zimbabwe in a desperate attempt to choke the country of badly needed outside funding.

Natives talk as if their President Mugabe is a crazy man. He very well may be. He has been in power for over twenty years and has become more of a dictator. His policies are not fair for all the people. He isolates himself, which goes against what he preaches. He hoards the wealth of the country and now murders it citizens, its white citizens. Even the enslaved blacks understand that murder is injust. The blacks that live in freedom in the city are plagued by corruption but at least they have risen above the lower class of people who have nothing. His land grabbing policies may destroy the Zimbabwe economy while the Brits hope their sanctions will crumble Zimbabwe's fragile, developing economy. Biased media will not let the truth be told. Do they want the world to know of these human rights issues? This economy is very fragile, could collapse and more blood will be shed. The British should turn back the pages of history and study it for they cannot maintain control. They tried embargos and sanctions against British colonies before, but the people could not be suppressed. Suppression does not stand in the way of freedom! The first British colonies that come to mind that overcame suppression and won freedom were located on the eastern shores of North America! There were thirteen of them. They now are part of the most powerful country on earth that stands united as fifty states.

The people of Zimbabwe will rise, succeed and win their freedom and dignity. We need to embrace and support them. The hell with the Mother Land; she must acknowledge her own wrongdoing. When I hunted in South Africa only seven years ago (1995), I was appalled at the fact that most blacks were still living in slavery. They could not eat with us and had to ride in the back of the pickup truck like a dog. They had won their supposed freedom under Mandela's rule, but remained enslaved. Their choice was be fed (and fed what no one else wanted to eat any way—animal entrails) or receive five dollars a month. They do not see television or hear the radio, so they think the white masters are a superior race and people. They are humble in front of you, but they are learning the truth. They too "will have a dream." They are not asking to have our wealth and material things. They just want to stand next to us as equals, as a person, as human beings. God is on their side. We had better be too if we want to stand next to them in the next world instead of gazing up at them from the firery gates of hell.

Frank Schmitz

The INNER FORCE

The Hunt Begins – June 1

Officially my hunt starts today. Once again sleep evaded me as I patiently wait for first light. I lay awake like a child on Christmas morning wanting to jump from bed and look at my presents, wrapped in decorative paper. Touch them, lift them, shake them and do the feely mealy thing. Such is the state of anticipation. What is anticipation anyway, I wonder?

This is a key word in hunting success and failure. The definition of anticipation according to Webster is "the act of anticipating or the state of being anticipated." If you don't know what anticipation means that definition tells you a lot of nothing, doesn't it? That would be like your son or daughter coming up to you and asking, "What is an orgasm?" And you would say, "Well that is the act of being orgasmic or the state of being organamistic." Ill bet they would say, "Oh now I understand; now it's perfectly clear to me." RRRight! So what is the definition of anticipate according to the good book. It is to realize or feel beforehand; forecast or foresee; to anticipate pleasure; to expect; to look forward to; wait in anticipation; expecting; hoping; to anticipate full-filling a life long dream; craving for the long awaited moment; to anticipate the expected; to be ready; to have rehearsed; practice acting; to have prepared for the moment; to have foreseen every angle; to be in complete readiness to only start to shake, to quiver, to melt down into a complete uncontrollable piece of shit. The definition of anticipations is – Buck Fever!

For all of us hunting nympho's who have laid in bed goggly eyed staring at the ceiling, listening to the clock - tick, tick, tick, tick, tick, waiting for the morning. We know what anticipation is.

My sleepless nights as a child where Christmas eve - wait a minute, I'll have to cut the crap right now! It was opening day of pheasant hunting and latter that fall, opening day of deer season. I was years too young to carry a gun, but I knew my brothers, cousins and I would soon be out stomping through corn fields and swamps with more enthusiasm than a good Labrador. Sleep - forget it! At 4:30 AM we gathered around the breakfast table our tongues hanging out, panting and drooling. Not because we were about to get a bowl of Coco-Puffs, but because we were about to go hunting. My dad would command, "Load up" as we scurried into the back seat of our 1965 Buick Wildcat, tails a wagging and

Frank Schmitz

glad we didn't have to be locked in the trunk with Uncle Bill's black lab. Soon we would be scouting through tall stalks of corn with mud caked boots, aimlessly zigging and zagging forward. Uncle Bill's whistle commands kept us in line as we forced the beautifully colored Asian pheasants ahead to the waiting guns at the field's last furrow.

Latter in fall we would stroll through swamps, beating sticks on trees and yelling as we fell into waist deep pot holes of icy water trying to force the mythical thirty point buck to our papas. The good old days, the glory days of anticipation. We had nothing to lose, only to anticipate.

As the teenage years come upon us, anticipation came with responsibility. Oh boy, the world trusted us with guns, and we had better be good. Mishandle, mis-aim, to not shoot, to shoot too often, to stumble or fall - all now came under heavy scrutiny by the elders.

If we screwed up - it was the death penalty, take away your gun and lose your fledging manhood. This responsibility thing and growing up isn't all its cracked up to be!

Now we lay awake at night, drooling less with a nervous tail waggle, wondering what if? What if the thirty pointer appears tomorrow! If I shoot it better be good. Then I will be raised atop my mentor's shoulders, held in high honor. I could be a god if I am calm, shoot clean and drop the thirty pointer. At about that time this little devil perks up on my shoulder. Hey super star! What if you screw up? What if you see the thirty pointer and you freeze. Shut-up you little bastard I think but he persists. What if you piss your pants, now what? Suupper ... Herroo!

I pull the pillow over my head and try to sleep. The thoughts run through my mind, if I screw up I will be an outcast, a joke. I'll be left behind next year. The little devil sits on my shoulder holding his thumb horizontal and fore finger vertical against his forehead - in the shape of a letter "L" while he chants loser, loser, loser.

The INNER FORCE

"How do I exorcise this little jackass?" I wonder as the song plays through my mind, "Anticipation." The lyrics play through my head "Anticipation is making me weak". We have all been there when anticipation hits - when buck fever over takes us. I made it until I was twenty-one before I succumb to anticipation. By then I had several deer under my belt and was actually gaining a reputation as a hunter in my little hamlet, tinker town or was it called Silver Creek? That year I decided to adopt a new sport,

Frank Schmitz

bow hunting. I was already a seasoned and cool killer with a gun. I had made it right through puberty without pissing my pants to having become successful at harvesting the wiley whitetail. This year I practiced nightly with my used Browning Cobra bow until I could hit a tomato 24 of out 25 times from anywhere in my yard. Surely William Tell could not hold a feather to my hat. My friends marveled at my archery ability. I was already a hero and I still hadn't even gone bow hunting. My first day I climbed high into a tree. Fifteen feet up was ok, but heck from thirty feet up I could see allot more. Once to that height, I thought, "Man, I can get up even eight more feet." Boy, now I can see everything. Whoppi!

Soon my experience paid off in selecting a good stand location between a swamp and an alfalfa field with a ripe white oak tree in the middle. Several does and fawns drifted to the natural candy stand as I watched with the eye of an eagle and the calm of a cougar waiting to pounce. "How cool would it be to kill a deer on the first day I ever bow hunted," I thought.

About then several deer started to meander right towards me. All right, here they come! As they closed in, suddenly my knees started to tremble. I thought to myself, "What the heck is going on, they're just doe's, I already had shot several bucks gun hunting." Then my knees shook uncontrollably as I started to panic. The song "anticipation is a making me weak" played in my mind. Oh my gosh! I realized I am getting buck fever! I grasped my legs and tried to quit panting like a rabid dog.

Mind over matter I preached to myself. Forget about the deer. Think about something like church or a nun whacking your fingers with a wooden yardstick. The little devil on my shoulder whispered into my ear, "You're not going to wet yourself, stud, are you!" I fought myself, exorcizing the little demon and finally cleared my mind, returning to calm. Then I looked around and wondered, "Where are the deer?" They vanished! Scanning the area - no deer, no deer, no deer. I looked straight down and there at the base of my tree stood the deer. "Ha, I got you now," I thought. A mere chip shot. I drew back, released and watched my arrow sail clear over the deer's back. They bounded off, blowing and snorting as if to say, "Everybody look at that fool way up in the tree. Hahahahaha, very funny." In my thousands of practice shots I never thought of shooting straight down. Yes, I now know, aim low! I had years of frustration with my bow, almost quitting the sport after losing a gut shot deer. Finally, I made a clean kill on

The INNER FORCE

an eight pointer. After that I shot only eight point or better bucks every year.

Anticipation is making me shake!

Buck fever is a good thing because that means we have dreams-goals-anticipation. Win, loose or draw, without anticipation hunting would be work. Those are the rewards of guiding. Many a deer, bear, lion or elk have fallen while I led a less capable man, not due to his physical attributes, rather due to his lack of knowledge of either or both the habits of our game and it's often complex landscape. Sharing others' success supercedes the act of accomplishment of personal harvest. I have celebrated in another hunter's glory often. That is the reward of a guide.

On the other hand I have lain awake in my tent replaying perfect stalks, perfect opportunity that went astray for my clients because of anticipation.

Their reactions vary from purely comical to violent. Everybody is different and we deal with our demons differently. I have had clients anxiously await a bugling bull, only gaze upon it when it appeared. These good-hearted fellows never even get mad or upset at lost opportunity. They rejoice in the magical moment. Others miss twenty-yard shots at big bulls and are a picture of pure frustration. They often blame their equipment, but when the equipment is still true they just get depressed. Yet others miss opportunity and get violently mad. Some want me to kill for them. Sorry wrong guy, wrong place, wrong time. I have seen it all, the good, the bad, the ugly. I have been it all too.

I just want to clarify to the addicted hunting world. God bless anticipation, as for Webster I think several words need to be re-defined.

NO.1# Hunting- the act of anticipation

NO.2# Anticipation- the act of buck fever

NO.3# Buck Fever- the act of understanding life; of being alive; the act of reaching puberty in the outdoors; the reason to exist; the reason for sleepless nights; the reason to dream; to explore; to taste the morning frost; to climb high; to hike far; to work and save to chase your dreams; to suffer in the cold; to risk financial stability; to follow your calling; to participate in tradition rituals that sustained our fore fathers, our human race. To feel alive and be alive to test our skills, survival skills, against mother nature. Buck fever, the blessed few that have felt its presence understand the definition of anticipation.

Frank Schmitz

My P.H. Nixon gathered me and my belongings up in a classic Land Rover. With him were Gravedigger and Bones, his son Steve and another fellow that I will call the Grim Reaper. We left Chiredzi to travel three hours south near the Gonarenhou National Park to a new location named Nyala Camp.

When we left, Nixon explained that the government set aside some land for people and some for animals. The road from Chiredzi to Harare was bursting with people. The game is gone, much like the buffalo on our great plains. It will never be back--that is history! But the area we travel to is for the animals and my faith in wild Africa was quickly restored. There were packs of baboon, several warthog, and impala along the road. I spotted a huge kudu bull off the road en route to camp. After arrival in camp, some eighty miles from a paved road, I was surprised to see a white woman—the first white person I had seen in a couple of days. She is the owner's aunt, Nancy, a third generation Zimbabwean. She assured me that she felt perfectly safe and that the uprising was winding down. I had never felt endangered enough to worry anyway. I explained I was not concerned and trusted my P.H. Nixon to do well!

The camp is in its first year of operation for Shanghi Safaris after having been abandoned several years ago. The previous outfitter had been gored nearly to death by a Cape buffalo and after two years of rehabilitation, decided to quit hunting. This camp is being restored and is very comfortable. They appointed a young black lady to see after my laundry and cleaning. She introduced me to the cook, Rosemarie. She grilled me on my likes and dislikes so that she would cook grub that I liked. (Not grubs - grub.) Nixon pulled out his old 375 H&H and said, "Let's see how you can shoot." The gun is an A-bolt action with a 1.5 x 5 Leopold. This is real similar to my gun "Dick" in London. The barrel has an end that looks like an old musket. It expands outward like a small funnel. The gun shot quite well at 100 yards.

This country is very different from what I expected. It is unlike South Africa where the land was rolling to mountainous with open savannas and timbered draws. This country is flat and densely vegetated. In South Africa, the game fled instantly and at longer distances. My average shot was 300 yards with many being 400 yards and beyond. Here the average shot I expect will be 50-100 yards and the game does not appear to be as spooky. Our primary hunting method is to creep down dirt trails with the Land Rover, trying to spot game.

The weather is unseasonably cold and raining lightly... very abnormal for this time of year. I said to Nixon that it is cool today! His reply was that this isn't cool; this is COLD! Bad for hunting. It may have been bad for hunting, but I saw impala, warthog, kudu, waterbuck, giraffe and eland in the afternoon. None were of trophy caliber, except a waterbuck that was monstrous. Nixon pleaded for me to shoot it, but I am not sure if I can pay the trophy fee for it unless I do not harvest some animals I am hoping for. My trigger finger itched immensely, but I passed him up. If other things go poorly, maybe I will see him again when my finger is uncontrollably twitching.

The afternoon turned toward dusk. Nixon was very concerned because I had not shot anything for leopard bait yet. We wanted to shoot some impala, but opportunity did not present itself. With less than forty minutes of light remaining, we moved down a lane in the Land Rover.

Nixon blurts out, "Shoot that pig, Frank, shoot that pig!"

I jump from the Land Rover with the trusty new piece, a 1960 375 H&H in hand as I see a dark silhouette vanishing in the underbrush. I sarcastically think to myself that is not a cop or an ill-mannered woman!, It still looks like a pig as I shoulder the 375. I hurry the first shot and follow it with a quick second round. The pig vanishes in the grass. "What the heck!" A 300-grain bullet from a 375 H&H and the damned pig is gone! How did I miss a 60-yard shot? Great shots you never forget especially at story time, but bad shots haunt you forever!

I was whitetail hunting with my brothers, Jeff and Tim, my Dad, and family friends, Todd Kultgen and John Friend. We had a ritual to hunt three small areas, which were called Tolentino's, Bittner's and Schueller's. They would be productive the first day or two but soon go south from outside hunting pressure. By the second to last day of the hunting season, we had enough of it by 11:00 a.m. It was noon in New York, so it was Miller time or Pabst Blue Ribbon time in our case. We commenced to drinking beer like starving pigs trying to suck a corn kernel out of a shit wallow! By midnight we were so drunk that we could not stand and piss anymore so we fell down and passed out wherever there was a soft spot at Tim's place. The next day we made it home. I was laying around feeling like I had a head-on collision with a freight train

Frank Schmitz

and killing time by watching the Green Bay Packers play whoop ass on the Tampa Bay Buccaneers, or in this case Flopeneers. It was Sunday....the last day of the hunting season. At about the fourth quarter of the game new life began to stir in me. I had to go back out hunting.

There were only a couple of hours of light left as I made my way into the Jackson Swamp. I had not gone far when I noticed a doe run over a rise. Wondering why it had run parallel with me after having spooked it, I realized that I had not spooked it. I edged forward until I could see over the rise. After studying the forest for several minutes, I made out a doe, a yearling fawn, and a rutting buck pursuing the doe. I played cat and mouse by following them until they passed through open swamp grass. With daylight diminishing rapidly, I only had time to follow them through the opening. As I walked into the clearing, the buck realized there was something on his back track. Perhaps he thought another buck was after his doe. He stepped from the brush at 100 yards, exposing himself to me. It was now that I first realized this was one of the biggest bucks I had ever seen, a 160-180 class, a true monster. I pulled up and started shooting until my five slugs were gone. I never hit him! I discovered my rear rifle site had come loose and was jumping around on the slide, meaning my aim was anywhere. I had just made the best stalk of my life only to be betrayed by faulty equipment. Things like that haunt you forever and should be lessons to learn. If your equipment is crap, you are crap.

Back in Africa, we are off and running looking left, right and straight ahead as darkness strangles the last light from the underbrush. There is movement and Nixon pats his hand on his shoulder while commanding shoot. I level the elephant gun across his shoulder while he plugs his ears. KAABOOOOM!! The first animal of my safari lies kicking on the ground with three holes in it. To my surprise all the shot's had been true, but the bullets had just zipped threw the wild pig without delivering any impact. Nixon congratulates me on the first bush pig killed in five years! He explains a warthog is very good eating, but bush pig is much better! We will eat like kings tomorrow.

A bush pig looks like a wild boar with long hair, an extra long snout and three-inch tusks sticking out of its upper and lower jaw.

The INNER FORCE

It is not pretty, but has not been as severely beaten with an ugly stick by our creator as the warthog. It is tan in color with a lighter tan color around its jaw and neck. My camera would not flash in the dark, so no pictures. What else? None-the-less, a rare and unexpected trophy! I was concerned by the fact that my bullets were ineffective in putting down this wild pig. Also, the full throw bolt smashed my thumb against the scope on the initial shot, delaying my reflex to shoot again. I had never used a full throw bolt.... a potential problem.

We returned to camp for a hearty dinner and white wine. Nancy's husband, Trevor, had arrived and the two of them are moving into this remote camp for now. He told me how his house in town was snake infested. They had found a half dozen deadly

Frank Schmitz

black mambas in their yard as well as two equally deadly cobras in their house.

They hate snakes, but who wouldn't. When bitten by a cobra you have twenty-four hours to live unless treated in South Africa were an antidote is available. If bitten by a black mamba, you have three hours to live unless you exert yourself. Then you will die more rapidly as the poison attacks your heart. The deceased famous African writer Peter H. Capstick wrote that if bitten by a black mamba while in the bush, his best advice for you is find the nearest cool shade tree; sit down, relax and enjoy that last hour of your life. After that, the discussion turned from poisonous scorpionsto the dreaded tsetse fly that bites you and lays its larvae under your skin. A week later when the maggots start to feed on your flesh you will see a tracking line develop where the bite occurred. The maggots grow feasting on your flesh and blood. At this point it is advisable to severe your skin in front of the track, push with your thumb and forefinger and squeeze them out of your body. Good way to get bait for fishing! From there, the conversation turned to how some four inch colored caterpillars as well as fried flying ants were good to eat. I decided it was bedtime and passed on the late night hors devours!

The INNER FORCE

Frank Schmitz

June 2

We rose at 5:30 AM to grab a little breakfast and set out. We still needed a kill for leopard baits. The day is dark and overcast. It is cold. This is the first cold snap of the year, the first days of winter in the Gonarozhou Range. Unlike elk hunting where cold, snow or rain means good hunting, here the thin skinned African game goes into hiding. Sunshine and warm weather is the recipe for success in Africa. The weather will change. It always does. Africa's abundance of game is due to the land's capability to sustain grass. In North America, elk and deer are thinly spread across wide areas in the summer because during the winter, ninety percent of the land has too much snow or no food. So the ten percent of the land that can sustain the game in winter represents the carrying capacity of the land. Here all the land has grass year around - either new grass or old. The carrying capacity of the land is one hundred percent, meaning this land can support ten times as many animals as the land I outfit on in Idaho.

The morning's cold definitely suppressed the game movement, as we saw no animals the first several hours. At about 9:30 AM, I spotted a critter to my right. As it turned, I identified it as a warthog - a very big warthog. Warthogs are the ugliest damned creatures on earth. They are animated looking creatures with big ugly warts protruding from their jaws and cheeks, like a cartoon character that gets hit on the head with a bat and a long high bump appears. That is the appearance of a warthog. They were severely beaten with the creator's ugly stick. This one had long curved tusks protruding upward from its snout. I grabbed the 375 and leveled it on him aiming in the center of the front shoulder, pushed off the safety and fired - misfire. Pushed the safety again and again. Where is the damned safety? I pull up to look for it. Damn, it's located on the side of the gun instead of over the stock. Since I was eighteen years old, my rifles' safety was on the stock and after twenty-seven years of shooting that's where my thumb goes. In the fifteen seconds of confusion of getting the gun ready to fire, the big pig disappeared in the bush. We tracked him for an hour but never caught up. Not having my gun cost me today, a similar mishap with an unfamiliar gun in the face of a leopard or buffalo could cost me dearly....indefinitely!

Frank Schmitz

It was not "day jua vu" as this tough looking pig disappeared into the jungle type foliage. Eight years prior, the gods were smiling upon me one clear sunny morning in South Africa. I was hunting with the world renowned Frank Bowker for plains game. I had managed to collect most of what I sought in that region and the time frame for hunting with him had come to an end. The remainder of the hunt was to be spent with Chappie Scott hunting for different species in a higher elevation. My hunting partner, Tommy Couch of Sanderson Texas, (whom by the way is the finest shot I know and has a heart the size of Texas) had already left to start hunting with Chappie.

I had asked if I could stay back one day extra for the sole purpose of trying one more time to harvest a wart hog. The odds were stacked high against me and we knew that it being a clear and sunny day they would head for the shelter of their burros early. We would need to have our stars come together in the first couple hours of light, by 8:30 AM we figured, if we were to be successful. At first light I found myself with Frank Bonker's son Merrick, my wife Terri and John Bull, our native tracker, slowly stalking and glassing from a rocky ridge top. It was a place were the semi-open savanna meet the rugged edge of the hill country. A place that could just as easily be west Texas as South Africa. It was cool - in the forties as first light stretched long shadows across the open savanna. Glassing light had been upon us for only fifteen to twenty minutes when Merrick spotted a respectable boar in the brushy edge of the foothills. We studied him for a while as he appeared and disappeared in the bush. Our main concern was that he might already be at or near the entrance to his underground bungalow. The warthog had disappeared for several minutes as we studied the underbrush for movement.

Then unexpectedly out of nowhere as if to be lady godiva proudly riding in on a white unicorn, a tremendous kudu bull came casually trotting onto the scene. Good Kudu bulls rarely present shooting opportunities. I had already harvested a very nice cape kudu, but these majestic beasts are something to behold. The bull was 450 yards below me as I dropped to my knees, bracing against a spindly bush. I never felt the report of my seven mag. However, I could see the mighty beast buckle as the 160-grain nozler tore threw his front shoulder.

"Shoot him again Frank," commanded Merrick.

The INNER FORCE

The magnificent seven spoke again as the grey ghost of Africa buckled and then collapsed to the baked clay floor of the savanna. High fives were in order. We all hustled down the mountain to inspect the glorious critter. His horns were good on a straight-line measurement but his spirals were exceptionally deep meaning he would score well. His cape and hide were flawless....a perfect specimen. After more backslapping and giggling we settled down to carefully stretch a tape from the base of his left horn through the deep spirals to its tip. Fifty and one quarter inches. We quickly decided to re-score it. The last fifty incher was shot by Frank Bowker himself when he was a lanky teenager. Forty-four years have passed since then. We re-scored knowing it was a rather simple measurement and we both are licensed master measurers. This time we ended up with fifty and one half inches. WOW! This kudu would be in the top twenty all-time, maybe top ten. What a morning. (It ended up at number 18 all-time although never entered into the record book).

John Bull decided to head for camp and round up the skinners. After a series of photographs we continued hunting down the ridge. Our sundials pointed at eight- o'clock and we knew the pigs were soon to be honkered down for the day.

We hustled back to the ridge top and headed north along its crest. The early movement of game had already ceased as we chugged along like the weary "I know we can locomotive." Hundreds of yards were behind us and nary hide nor tail of a living creature as we pressed on like the " I think we can locomotive." Mickey Mouse's hand pointed at nine o'clock. Sweat broke across our foreheads as the sun pushed higher into the morning sky. We could feel her heat intensify against our tender pink skin as we carried on glassing and searching. Soon the clock struck ten. Our odds of finding pumba were all but nil. Yet we pushed fourth like the "I thought I could locomotive."

As I brushed sweat from my brow with my forearm I caught a flash of movement at about a hundred yards ahead at the three o'clock position. It was nearly 10:30 when the tell-tale sign appeared.

"Did you see that?" I yelped to Merrick.

"Ya, bushbuck?" Was his questioning response.

I had seen the animated tail, a tail being carried straight vertical from the ground. In a manner that only a Kottamonde of South America would do - or a warthog of Africa.

Frank Schmitz

I replied "No, I seen a warthog or at least a warthog's tail".
"Are you sure?" Merrick questioned.
"Positive!" I responded.

We quickly started to glass for the fast moving pig. Instantly he appeared in on opening three hundred yards below us. In the minute and a half of our conversation he had already covered over two hundred yards. I dropped to a prone position, braced my elbow on my knee and leveled the rifle as pumba disappeared into the bush. In the next instant he darted into a small opening at 350 yards as my A bolt barked out.

My concentration was on ejecting a spent cartridge, reloading, and taking aim as Merrick bellowed, " Unbelievable! That was an unbelievable shot! He is down!".

Surprising myself, I just looked at him and said, "Really?"
"Oh yes, he is busy dying in that draw!"

In short order we descended the mountainous hillside and soon stood beside the powerful, ugly, yet comical looking beast.

Merrick explained "Man he is a whopper. This is a huge pig. He must be one of the first we ever let go when we introduced them in the area."

I obviously did not know a whopper when I'd seen one. Instead I admired his worn tusks and fondled his long rubbery protruding warts. "What a strange creature," I thought.

Later, back at the ranch, to appease Merrick's curiosity we scaled the hog. He tipped in at 204 pounds, a new record for the Bowker ranch, the biggest ever. Talk about a day. This certainly had been my best day ever as a hunter. I could not help but reflect on the fact that if we would have left as scheduled this day would never have come to pass. Perseverance pays off. It is a shining example of the "never quit, I know I can" attitude that separates glory and failure.

But today is different. It's a different time, a different place, a different gun, and for me, for the first time in years a different frame of mind. Not a good one either!

I hate it when I am guiding and a client cannot shoot his gun. With the tables turned I must say I felt embarrassed and a little humiliated. Gravedigger and Bones were scratching their heads in wonder. What is wrong with our Bwana (Great White Hunter)? I missed this warthog without ever firing a shot. I simply fumbled around with the unfamiliar safety and gun, while blowing the chance at a very good warthog. The remainder of the morning was uneventful except for the sighting of the two giraffes. I am a little concerned that we have not seen spoor of buffalo or sable and only one leopard track to date. I am also concerned that my ammo, 300-grain solids, for stopping buffalo is not very effective on other game because it just zips a pinhole in them like an arrow would. These are definitely unexpected challenges that will affect the outcome of this adventure.

It is mid-day. The animals rest so we head for camp to take a siesta, too. I kick off my rags and boots and crawl into bed, determined to catch up on my sleep. Before I left for this trip, I was helping my friend (Boyd Hopkins) stucco a house during the day and worked until midnight on our gift shop we were preparing to open called "The Summit Trade 'N Post". It will feature artwork, paintings, metal work, antler art and woodcarvings. Terri and I worked eighteen hours a day to get it ready including working through the night until dawn before I left.

I fell into a deep sleep, but knew that we must be up within the hour. I heard some noise at my door half-past the hour. I thought it might have been open. Still mostly asleep I felt the covers pull back behind me and I struggled to awaken. My legs and arms felt like they were filled with lead and my body felt as if I was drugged. I wrestled with my mind to awaken and move. I felt the soft warm body of a full breasted woman press up against my back. Stricken with the panic of a high school virgin, I struggled to turn and face the invader. As I managed to roll over, a soft gentle hand rubbed up my loins toward the royal crown. My face was met by moist warm lips being pressed against my mouth, embracing me in a deep kiss! As my mind and eyes focused, I realized it was my gorgeous wife, Terri. My body flooded with joy as my mind raced, "How did you get here?" What a surprise, I thought, as I hugged her imagining only of engaging in copulation.

Then there was a knock at the door. Not now!. The knocking came again. This time with a voice. "Bwana, it is time to go, Bwana."

My dream interrupted, I replied, "Huh" as I shook my head to full consciousness and reality. Damn you Bones! Why did you wake me now! I ought to punch you in the nose, but then realized if he had not waked me that wonderful dream would have been lost in my mind forever. The reality was that I was still in Africa.

I jumped up to grab my boots. I for the first time felt alone. I am on the opposite side of the world from everyone I know; in

Frank Schmitz

a different land and culture and hemisphere. It is weird tothink about it. It was time to get out on our next quest for fate. The day remained overcast and dreary with little animal movement.

The night before, Nancy's husband, Trevor, told me that Nixon saved the company owner's life twice. Once from a lion charge and once from the wrath of a leopard. I did not want to ask him about the details of those encounters but instead elected to ask him if he had experienced any close encounters with game.

Nixon replied in his fluent, but yet broken English, "Ahh a few in the last couple years. Three years ago a lion charged me and last year a buffalo took my gun away. Then there wasthe client that got attacked by a leopard!"

I responded with a surprise, "A client was attacked by a leopard? How did that happen?"

Nixon responded, "Frank, when you shoot the leopard be sure to take both lungs, and a buffalo...you must break both shoulders. Then we are good! If you break one, if he comes on three legs, he will get you! The client shot his leopard and broke one shoulder. The leopard just vanished. We spread out to search in the grass. It was open but suddenly the leopard appeared from nowhere! Just from nowhere, I am telling you! The client was a very big man, 6'5", 260 pounds, but the leopard charged and knocked him down like a piece of paper! He just went down like that, BAM. He got his arm up but the leopard bite on it and then run into the bush! So, I go after him. The next thing I know the crazy thing charges me, but I finish him. It was the first time I take client to the hospital".

"Another time this P.H. I know who owned Walkabout Safaris was elephant hunting. It was twenty-one day hunt and they hunted hard for three weeks, no elephant. It is the last day and they are leaving when he spots an elephant. The client and trackers decide to go closer and check it out. They sneak closer and closer to where the elephant was but no elephant. Then just like that the elephant lets out a scream and appears. The Bwana sends the P.H. and trackers running up the hill and he jumps into the riverbed and starts running. I do not know why but I guess to distract the elephant. The elephant charges him down and takes him through the back. His tusk, he drove it through his back and comes right out his chest. He died instantly. Two years ago in Zambia the same thing. A client from Florida is hunting with his P.H. when an elephant screams and charges out of nowhere! The

P.H. dodges to the side, as the elephant goes after the client. The client runs for his life but the elephant is right on him. The P.H. tries to get a backside brain shot at him. He shoots the elephant but the elephant collapses right on the client, crushing him. Frank, I am telling you these animals are dangerous. It is not easy"! Nixon pauses, shaking his head.

We spot a warthog – too small; impala – no bucks; waterbuck – all cows. Then darkness overtakes the savanna and we head for camp. Tomorrow — it is another day.

Tonight I will sleep with my gun and practice with the full throw bolt, safety and aiming. I must get intimate with this weapon if it will perform for me! This hunt has pitted me against my own practical advice. One - Know your weapon. Two - Match the ammo to the game. Three - Low power optics beats higher power. I like a 1.5 X 5 power scope. This weapon strikes out for me. I will have to adjust and overcome. A disturbing trend I have noticed is people keep buying bigger scopes with larger objective lenses. People tend to think bigger is better but to the contrary, field of view is most important. The smaller the power of the scope, the larger the field of view. You can't shoot on animal you can't see in your scope. In thick bush 3 and 4 power is too much scope for fast shots. It's worse yet if your scope is turned up to 12 or 14 power. Remember, an animal is just as far away whether you are looking at it at 1.5 power or 14 power.

Anyway, I will befriend this stranger. I had better. The chatter of a monkey calls out from the darkness outside. I wonder if he laughs at the pale skinned one with his funny weapon sitting in the screened-in shelter of my hut. I blow out my candle, thinking "Haaa, you can't see me any more!"

Frank Schmitz

June 3

Today we hope that these early days of winter will break and the sun will return to Africa. The days are short with sun up at 6:30 a.m. and sundown at 5:30 p.m. My wife is a very thoughtful person whom likes to organize and plan. Me, I shoot from the hip. I just wing it, taking things day to day. For instance even though I had booked this trip four years ago, I did not pack a thing until the day before I had to leave. I did not get around to shooting the U.K.M. (my 7 mm) until the morning I was leaving. Terri, on the other hand, had cards in envelopes for everyday I was gone; dated, in order, and hid in my luggage that I was still packing the day I was leaving. In the past twenty-three years, she and I have only been apart once for this long, so I find myself thinking of her more and more often. I look forward to my next card and appreciate her thoughtfulness. I wonder how she is and if my daughters have arrived at my home yet. Our oldest, Angie, and youngest, Melissa, were coming to visit her with our grandchildren, Trey and Samantha. I know Terri is busy running our lodge and store and tending to our dogs, cats, goats, chickens, ducks, geese and whole team of twenty plus horses.

I slept from 10:30 PM until 4:00 AM. and now lay awake waiting for the rest of Africa to awaken. Nixon explained to me it is very critical to shoot something today because we have to get the leopard baits started. One of Nixon's assistants has already killed and hung several baits in a concession (?) on the big parks border about one-hundred miles from here. It is a better leopard spot and my chance at a strike there will be greater. If we get our baits, we will leave here in a day or two and travel to another area to hunt buffalo.

Do you every wonder what makes us do what we do?

Why do we want to be a Doctor or Lawyer? Why do we want to collect do-dads and thing-a-ma-jigs? Who knows! But I do know I was a collector of wildlife from little on. I started out collecting bugs, butterflies and moths as a toddler. My passion slowly grew to reptiles, amphibians and fish. Then to small game and birds and finally to collecting big game species. I would like to share a story that took place somewhere between third to fifth grade if memory serves me correctly. Some names had to be changed to protect the innocent (or more properly stated, guilty).

Frank Schmitz

Anyway at about that age I discovered tiger salamanders. These shiny, smooth skinned amphibians really turned my clock. We had no clue where they came from but we sure knew how to catch the elusive little beasts. It seemed that these miniature dinosaurs would appear during the night, slither around doing whatever salamanders do and inevitably fall into someone's basement window well. So on most any sunny summer day my older brother Mike, running mate from diapers on, Rick Thome and I would sneak from house to house inspecting window wells for salamanders and other bonus creatures, like toads, frogs and snakes. We would raid fruit trees and gardens along the way to sustain ourselves. Unpopular with the elders I might add.

As one can imagine, an operation like this required extreme caution, nerves of steel and Olympic speed. Naturally we were sworn to silence, even "In the face of bodily harm" because a valuable secret like this could never get into the enemies' hands. Extreme caution was paramount when approaching and inspecting window wells. We did not want anyone to see us and catch on to this form of trapping, especially neighbor kids and housewives. Speaking of housewives, this is where the nerves of steel requirement came in because it seemed some of these misguided soap opera gazers thought that we were trying to break into their basements. Many of these old hags could be wicked. I knew all to well that the peaceful church going young ladies as well as grannies on our little town's block had a dark side.

I had overheard my dad talk about them at the supper table and knew danger lurked in the neighboring yards. When things were really bad, mom and dad spoke in the old world tongue "Luxemburg" so we would not learn too much. But when fine women of the neighborhood were referred to as "Battle Ax", "Hatchet Face" and the most feared of all, "Stinky Pete," we knew we had better watch our backs! Who would want to be caught in a headlock under the armpit of a women referred to as "Stinky Pete?" Obviously survival instincts needed to be learned and applied if we were to flourish. Sometimes the old hags would lay and wait for us, trying to dump or spray water on us or even worse, crack us with their brooms. This is where Olympic speed came in handy. Yes, this endeavor was definitely for the brave of heart. One day as we were strolling home after a successful morning of harvesting frogs, toads and salamanders we met a fellow kid coming our way on the side walk. This kid's name was

The INNER FORCE

Tom Sinner and he was a robust young lad, literally popping at the seams. As he waddled towards us lapping peanut butter out of a jar with one of his plump fingers we tried to hide our bucket of critters behind us. Tom's eyes were to sharp however and he soon inquired "What's in the bucket"?

Rick responded, "Nothin."

"Let me see," Tom demanded.

Well, we were afraid of being sat on so I said, "You have to promise to keep it a secret."

"Keep what a secret?" Tom asked

"What's in the bucket you dummy>. Rick added.

Tom gave in and said, "OK, but it better be good."

So we showed him the treasures, three frogs, one toad, and four salamanders.

"Cool, where did you get them?" Tom shouted.

"It's a secret," I told him. "We caught them in a secret spot."

After ten minutes of arguing, Tom's interest became directed to the bucket.

"Hey did you ever see a frog stick his tongue out?" Tom asked

We all looked puzzled and said, "No." With that Tom stuck his pudgy little hand into the bucket grabbing a leopard frog, pulling it out and raising his arm high above his head. Then with all the force he had in him, he thrust his arm down, letting go of the frog, thus smashing him on the concrete sidewalk. He started laughing robustly, pointing at the frog. "Look at him, his tongue is sticking out." We stood there horrified at what he had just done. Our moms had told us there were bad people in the world but this was cold-blooded murder. I had only heard of one act more hideous than this, that being a story of a couple of brothers who claimed to having caught frogs would stick a straw up their poopers and blow them full of air. Once blown up like a helium balloon, they would toss the frogs into the creek where they bobbed around on the surface. While pretending they were enemy battle ships they would shoot them with their BB guns and watch them explode. Sick O's! I can hear the dueling banjos playing or is it the theme song for "Cisco the Kid." Tom started reaching for the bucket, "Give me another frog," he demanded.

It was time for our Olympic speed to kick in. We grabbed up the pail and dashed off. No wonder his name was Tom Sinner. We must be more cautious in the future. We took our amphibians

Frank Schmitz

home and released them into our big sand box where we had excavated tunnels and built moats as well as sand castles. Here the critters could frolic around in our little Disney world setting; swimming, climbing, or hiding out.

One day the Gonwa boys showed up; Itchy, Scratchy and Dork. These guys were sure to be nothing but trouble. We knew they would soon claim half our trap line if the truth was told and we did not need competition like this. In latter years, Itchy(Larry) would be the best man at my wedding. I was the same for his. I would stand up for Scratchy's (Ronnie) wedding and become close friends with Dork (Dan) who really was the sharpest of the bunch. We ended up being birds of a feather, but were adversaries for now.

Itchy asked, "Where are you guys getting all those lizards?"

Rick responded with extremely quick thinking, "In Ollie Arndt's field." We knew all about Ollie Arndt, a decrepit old bugger with a nasty disposition. He had a farm next to town and a pond that we had already checked out. He hated trespassers and would come storming out of his old house with a shotgun, bellowing at us. Several times he shot below our feet as we ran for our lives. A wicked old geezer he was.

The Gonwa boys questioned "Really? They are just crawling around in the field?"

"Yep," we responded and they were off running towards Ollie's field wearing their brand new little leather work boots. Well, old Ollie Arndt's field was plowed up and was nothing but oozing mud. It seems that after they got to floundering around in his field, and after good old Ollie started shooting over their heads, these boys lost interest in salamanders. As a matter of fact, once they cleared the last furrow in Ollie's field they were minus five brand new work boots. Going back to look for their shoes while facing the wrath of the old geezer's gun was out of the question. Going home to face mom was perhaps more dangerous. She did not see the humor in these mud covered, shoe less boys when they got home. They were last seen sitting on the front porch like the "hear no, see no, do no evil monkey's" with properly tanned behinds waiting for dad to come home. Oh Boy!

Well, the word was out! We had a sandbox full of never before seen salamanders and they came from Ollie Arndt's field. After the Gonwa boys failed at their attempt at catching some, nobody in town dared risk their lives going over there. We had cornered the

The INNER FORCE

market, but like with all good things either the government or the underworld is going to come and get you. In our case it was the underworld. There was a pair of overgrown neanderthal's called the Sitterbugger's. They were twice as big and strong as anybody in town. That made them at least three times bigger than me. I was a late bloomer, small for my age. Worse yet, my older brother Mike was even smaller. Mike was very sick with asthma and particularly stunted in growth. He left the collecting of critters up to Rick and me most time while he designed and sculpted the sand box.

On the day of reckoning Mike and I were busy playing with our salamanders when suddenly a shadow cast over me. I looked around to see the Sitterbugger boys, "Billy the bugger" and his mammoth brother "Mike the menace." The conversation started out with Billy saying, "Heard ya found them lizards in Ollie Arndt's field."

"Yep." I replied.

"We didn't see anything over there." Mike the menace added.

"Probably hibernating." I told him.

"Well then how about you give us some of yours?" Billy said.

"Sorry they are not for sale!" I told them.

The menace then shoved me to the ground and said, "Well we're taken them!" as he and Billy started to gather up our prize pets.

I jumped up and socked Big Mike in the belly, which was just enough to make him drop our critters so he could grab me by the neck and start choking me. I helplessly tried to pry his meat hooks from my neck as I gagged. It was no use, I was dead meat! Suddenly I heard a loud "Bong" and mighty Mike drops to his knees. Behind him standing on a bucket is my little big brother holding a metal sand shovel in his hands. It seems he had just administered the steel shovel to the top of big Mike's head with every thing he had in him. Big Mike knelt on the ground in from of me, holding his head. He was balling like a baby while he yelled out, " He hit me." Turns out big Mike, whom was gifted with size and strength, he had just learned an important lesson in life. Although he could intimidate his fellow man with size, Sampson can beat Goliath! This is something we all have to learn to grow into a better human being and person. This so unnerved Billy the bugger that he dropped his salamanders and started to run for home. Soon Mike

Frank Schmitz

the menace was up and running after him. Somehow we managed to protect our stock, until the leaves started to turn colors and fall winds whispered to us that winter was around the corner. It was time to let the critters go so they could hibernate. But, the Indiana Jones in me was already deeply entrenched!

I had a Huck Finn childhood for sure with countless hours spent fishing in my hometown lake, Random Lake, Wisconsin. We spent hours catching crawfish, turtle's or anything that could crawl, slither or just plain moved. Day trips took us by way of railroad tracks to neighboring lakes, streams and wood lots to hunt, fish and explore. There was no time for T.V. Thank God video games and computers had not yet been invented. I surely wouldn't want to be growing up in the present day and age.

My day dreaming of my youth was interrupted as Nixon's voice returned me to the reality of the Dark Continent. The commander and chief said, "Buffalo—it is not easy—it will take time."

We must track them into the bush, heavy bush, so that is the game plan. We are definitely building a friendship as Nixon confides in me with family and business matters. Yesterday, when we came to a fork in the trail, Nixon asks me, "Which way?" Neither fork appeared to offer an advantage over the other.

Without thinking, I respond, "Ini-mini-miney-mo, catch a Ni--", oops. I look at him as he looks at me and a deep hearty laugh breaks out as I join in.

"Let's go left," Nixon says!

Politically incorrect is politically correct in Africa. Why is it wrong to call a spade a spade or a heart a heart, or a club a club? Why must we call it a card? If the truth is offensive to someone, is it still not the truth! You can bet my stupid honky white ass it is and that does not offend me in the least, thank you.

This morning it looks as if old man winter's icy grip on Mother Africa's throat is subsiding. The clouds are breaking and surely there will be blood on the forest floor if the sun shines!

We head out at daybreak, driving for an hour, but nothing is moving in the savanna. We decide to turn towards the river. One-half mile away a Jurassic creature feeds on the treetops like he has for fifteen or maybe twenty years. He has seen his last dawn as a pack of the most feared predators in the forest amble his way. There are six dark-skinned ones and one light-skinned. They carry with them sticks cast of iron and wood; one they call 375 and the other 416.

The INNER FORCE

   For this magnificently animated beast perhaps it is this magnificent beast's lucky day for his death will come fast and clean; not like it does most times. Most times death is slow and cruel. Mother Nature is not kind when she wields her sword of death by starvation, sickness and predation. This creature wears the jungle scars of reality on his neck, forehead and wounded front hoof, but has perservered to be a dominant bull of his species. Unknowingly to the towering creature, the blue-eyed one has taken aim on his chest. The fire pole speaks as the fair-skinned one struggles to inject another round – his thumb caught between the full throw bolt and its scope. I remember shooting this huge brut and as I lowered the gun to eject the shell I fully expected the shock of the shot to kick his ass back to his mother's womb! I thought he would stagger like a drunk on Bourbon Street, falling to his bed like he had just made a deal with a ten-cent whore! The animal never flinched! Instead, it started trotting off in an animated, rocking lope. The dark-skinned ones were on him like a pack of mad wolves, running after him through the towering brush. Soon we were upon him again and shortly a volley of lead penetrates the great beast, this time from both guns. His towering legs wobbled and caved inward, collapsing into himself like one of the twin towers tumbling to earth. The eighteen foot tall creature crumbles to the ground. The blue-eyed one quickly put a "Coup de Grace" into his neck. Life has ended for the two and one-half ton beast. The gunner had killed tremendous beasts before, a bull moose with a sixty-inch rack in Dease Lake, British Columbia. That huge beast weighed 1400 pounds. Several years later in South Africa he had toppled an eland that weighed nearly a ton. But never had he stood before a beast of this size and magnitude.
   A beautiful beast, a seemingly peaceful creature – in spite of his heavily scarred head which showed signs of brutal battles with others of his species. The dark-skinned predators swarmed over this beast like a joyous pack of wolves while the fair-skinned one stood by feeling dirty – feeling soiled.
   As the humans gathered around the beast, the blue-eyed Bwana struggles with himself to justify what he has done. For a full hour he admires the great beast with a heavy heart. He feels no joy or satisfaction while the others feel no pain or sorrow. They are not as far removed from reality in the life and death cycle. They have no Disney World misconceptions. Finally the fair-skinned

Frank Schmitz

one comes to grips with what he's done. He has provided a ton of meat for his assistants and their families, enough for 4,000 servings. He has saved the lives of at least a dozen or perhaps twenty other creatures; other creatures that would have had to die to feed this local human population. These other creatures now have a temporary extension on their life tickets. The beast will be utilized in its entirety. What is not cut up for human consumption will be placed as bait where other predators will dine on it, invariably sparing the lives of yet some other creatures. If a predator is in turn harvested off the meat, yet countless more critters' lives will be spared. The back cape will be made into seat coverings and rugs, the feet into table legs and the head into a re-creation of the majestic beast....to be gazed upon in honor. Even the blood that has spilled into the ground will nurture new life by sustaining grass for yet other creatures. Such is the life cycle that we are all part of - "ashes to ashes, dust to dust" - none of us can escape the reality of Mother Nature. In spite of all that, I will never shoot another giraffe.

The INNER FORCE

The beast is butchered in its entirety right on the spot and transported to camp. When we leave, the only sign of an animal passing is the blood stained ground, the matted down grass and the turds that have been stripped from its intestines. The natives took everything that I did not want – meat, bones, hide, all the organs, all the guts, including all the stomach contents. People who grow up poor and hungry do not waste the high protein of organs and high fat content of intestines and stomach.

Frank Schmitz

I have long realized nothing is wasted in nature as coyotes and crows quickly strip every last bit of flesh we leave behind at an elk kill. But here even the jackals and vultures do not get a free meal, competing with humans for the last bite. The butchering of a giraffe was a challenging ordeal made more difficult by the fact that a giraffe is perhaps the thickest-skinned critter to walk the planet. Its hide is at least a full one inch thick – maybe an inch in a half. Skin that thick is difficult to turn and peel back not to mention the skinners knives are nothing more than a kitchen butcher knife. They periodically sharpen them with any old rock lying on the ground. You just know there is no edge on these knives yet they manage to accomplish the task at hand. Truly amazing!

On the way to camp we see bushbuck, warthog, waterbuck and baboon. The jungle is alive as the sun warms her face.

As I was writing this journal, I looked up to see a family of baboons watching me from nearby. They have been growing tolerant of us and seem to be becoming increasingly curious. Unlike monkeys that are cute and comical, these baboons look menacing. They have an evil appearance about them and it makes me wonder if the bad people of this earth come back as baboons.

The afternoon was spent placing leopard baits. We used two of the lower front shoulders of the giraffe, wiring them into trees along river locations. Then chunks of the giraffe guts were dragged in circles from the bait sites to create scent trails while Bones spread stomach content along the trail.

This would simulate a kill - making a leopard follow it to the meat believing it had found another animal's kill. We will check the baits daily from here on in for a strike. If and when a strike occurs, we will build a grass blind on location and wait to see if the leopard returns. At the second location I was scouting along the river for spoor and located a leopard track that Nixon verified as a large foot print. That was promising indeed. On the flip side, cloud cover moved back in and like flipping a light switch, the earlier heavy game movement seized. We saw no game this afternoon. Tonight we gorged ourselves on bush pig, a very tasty treat, washing it down with South African wine. On my way to my room I intercepted the pesky baboons nosing around. They had better be careful or they will be a target species.

Trevor, the white Zimbabwean, returned today without Nancy whom I assumed stayed in town. He brought along the paper which I noticed Nixon reading. The big front-page headlines read,

The INNER FORCE

"White Farmer Shot Dead." I did not ask, but it is apparent civil unrest is ongoing in the countryside.

The safari operator told me civil unrest was in outside areas far from where we would be. This is not true because the blacks pointed out many areas occupied by squatters. Yet they are careful to protect you from seeing too much. They did not want you to see unrest or feel threatened. That is obvious. Where ever I have been, the people of the countryside are open, honest, trusting and giving. I think that is true here, but one should be very cautious in the city, Harare, or any city that is unfamiliar I guess.

As noted before, the first day here I had to offer a reward to get my stolen folder and passport back at the airport. Later at the hotel, I was approached by a friendly woman who, after a brief conversation, asked if I wanted to escort her to her apartment for coffee. I declined, but the next black woman to approach me, very well endowed and dressed scantily, started a conversation with me.

I did not doubt her intentions so I said, "I am married!"

She replied, "You come with me, I don't have to f-ck you. I can give you a very nice massage."

Yah right! Probably drug me and rob me and give me AIDS to boot. The next morning I went to the open market across the street. I wanted to purchase a carving but needed Zimbabwean money. They sent me by a man to exchange my cash for the correct change. As we exchanged the money, four men charged into me, knocking me down and blocking me as I tried to grasp the Zimbabwean cash with one hand while my hundred dollar bill was stripped from my other hand. As they fled away they were ninety dollars richer. I got up, brushed myself off, thankful to be unharmed (besides my pride). I did lose some faith in humanity that morning, feeling extremely violated. So much so that I neglected to record this story earlier. After being mugged I was feeling somewhat like a rape victim. I returned to the security of the Meikels hotel. I realized that I was just no more than a foolish country boy in a big city where corruption is survival.

Cities here as everywhere create opportunity, spawn greed and corruption, breed mistrust and rob people of decency. Cities optimize the devolution of mankind - changing honest, trusting and good people into disillusioned survivalists. I do not begrudge my attackers. I pity them. So within the first twelve hours of arriving in the big city, I had opportunity to be mugged, robbed

Frank Schmitz

and raped. Of course the British took my guns but offered to return them if I was willing to let them blackmail me.

At the end of this hunt, I will see if the government is enforcing some sort of marshal law. Police have six roadblocks set up between Harare and Chipenshi. On the way to camp we encountered additional roadblocks here in Cheridzi. The police (all black men) always waved us through. I assume they did so because they saw me and figured I was a tourist. I asked Nixon and another local about the roadblocks, since they seemed to be inspecting black men's trucks and cars. Nixon said they were checking for speeders. I asked how you would check for speeders when we stop at roadblocks and they have no radar or equipment. What was going on? I do not know but I suspect that there is a movement building in Zim for a political overthrow and the government is trying to suppress this action.

Mugabe, the president, has a policy of returning this land to the people. He is extremely popular, but has severely crippled Zimbabwe's economy and world standing. First of all, the takeovers were violent, stealing white-owned family farms. At least twelve farmers have been killed. There is no compensation to the white farmers and even the poor blacks realize the unsuitable acts of murder are unacceptable. This has forced many white farmers to leave the country – the land squatters have no money – can't operate equipment or irrigate – meaning no crops have been planted. Now the population is faced with extreme shortages, high prices and starvation. Most folks will find freedom a painful and unrewarding transition in their lives.

Life is different when you leave U.S. air space and in many parts of the world a lone white man is an obvious target for greed. There is safety in numbers, but it stretches your balls out a little when you have to stand alone among some people whom are as fond of white skin as the Klu Klux Klan is of black skin.

We live in a less than perfect world, but as Americans, we can stand tall. In spite of our own shortcomings we lead the way on this planet for equality and human rights. For that we should always be proud to be an American.

June 4

I woke at 4:30am after six and one-half hours of sleep, a personal record to date. I imagine in another week I will be sleeping like Nixon would say, "a dead log." It is cold in the room this morning and I wonder what the weather will be today. My gun problems have continued. The large warthog was missed because I could not find the safety. After shooting the giraffe in the boiler room, it never even flinched.

The 300 solids just zip pin holes in the animals. I recovered one of the tips. There is no expansion whatsoever, so the animals absorb no shock. My 7 mag would tear into them with a nozler. Worse yet, the full throw bolt on the sako caught my thumb between the bolt and the scope, wedging it tightly thus jamming my gun. My follow-up was ten times slower than with my A-bolt. I remember that when I shot the bush pig, I smashed my thumb against the scope trying to inject the second round also. Man this gun just kills me, or at least it could!

Old man winter is back, raping Mother Africa. The skies are clear but cold. Frost is a rare thing this close to the equator but it is close to freezing this morning. I wish I had gloves now. Old man winter demands respect from mother nature!

Last time I came to Africa, I had trouble shooting the first couple days. It is intimidating when there is an entourage of people watching you and you can't judge the animal's distance because you don't understand its size. But when my shooting shoes came on in the third day I was blessed to put on a display of unparalleled marksmanship unparalleled to any I or most anyone else had ever seen. It is unlikely I will ever get that hot again. I was in an unconscious state while shooting several animals at 300 to 400 yards, without good rests or off-hand. I also harvested half dozen others in the 250-300 yard range. When I left, the professional hunters told me that Tommy Couch (my hunting partner and a true marksman) and myself had put on the best shooting display they had ever seen. We replied that we would be talking about this hunt for years! To which they respond, NO; we will be talking about you two for years - especially the 600-yard off-hand shot, the best I have ever seen! Sometimes having had such gratifying success can haunt you. My personal expectations are to re-achieve this feat, but like a championship team trying

Frank Schmitz

to repeat, it is harder to remain focused. It is more difficult to maintain the inner force after experiencing unparalleled success. Like a team ravaged by free agency departures, the player's that are left must step-up and overcome their handicaps, dig deeper to succeed.

When I become unconscious with my shooting, it is a reflection of confidence more so than skill. Whenever I have made long shots at running game anyone around me always asks, "How did you hold, how high, how much did you lead him?" But I never know the answer! I never remember how I held, even right after the shot because it is instinctive! When you're shooting instinctively, you do not think about anything. You just know when it is time to pull the trigger. I believe that you can actually think the bullet to the animal. It's a leap of faith. You have to feel the force if you will! The only way to reach that unconscious state is to have complete confidence in your equipment. You have to be familiar and fluent with your gun. You have to know the gun is dead on. You have to understand your bullet's trajectory. The gun must fit you so that it is an extension of your body and mind. Obviously on this hunt not having my own weapon is a huge obstacle to overcome. I have no spare ammunition to practice with. The stock is short. The scope does not fall to my eye. The safety is in the wrong place and the throw on the bolt is too high. The ammo is ineffective. Boy, I wish I had my A-Bolt, but you know the saying, "You can wish in one hand and shit in the other and all you will have is a handful of warm shit."

The day is clear as we head out. Dixon (Bones), Nixon (P.H.), his son Steven, the Grim Reaper and I come across a good warthog but I fumble around trying to get a rest and he disappears. I feel the pressure to shoot faster and soon have the chance as we relocate the pig. This time I hurry my shot as the pig bolts. I shoot him in the ass and jam the spent cartridge without clearing it, ruining any chance of a follow-up shot. We set out tracking and after a long while find a couple specs of blood. Soon that dries up and tracking conditions are near impossible. When about all appears lost, Bones whistles for my attention. I hurry over to his location and see the big boar standing in some brush. His head is exposed as I drop behind it shooting into the brush. I know a 300 solid can break a few twigs and hit the animal. As the pig bolts out I clear the chamber and reload fluidly for the fist time but do not have time for a follow-up shot. There is new blood, however,

The INNER FORCE

and it gets heavier as we go. I think to myself, well it's the same as if I had shot him with an arrow - a quick pinhole, but we will have him soon. The trick is on me once again as the blood trail dries up. Nixon and Bones question me on the shot. "Frank, are you aiming for the front shoulder or the butt? You have to shoot in the front shoulder. You must aim!"

How fricken embarrassing is this. Me, a professional outfitter and guide. A seasoned hunter and quite experienced I may add, getting grilled as if it was my first day in hunter's safety class. We track and track, finally more blood. My hopes soar that I will save face, but for the third time, it dries up. Three hours later we throw in the towel.

This is the first animal I have ever hit and not recovered in Africa. We travel on seeing jackal, a civet cat and cheetah. All critters I would love to harvest, but did not get a shooting opportunity at any of them. And then a large impala appears in an opening at 150 yards.

Nixon instructs, "Take him Frank."

I draw a bead on him, squeeze the trigger and watch the antelope crash to the ground. FINALLY, I think to myself. Finally an animal shows some response to being hit, as I hear Bones say to Nixon in African, "He spined him."

The big impala lays, kicking on the ground as we head for him. Suddenly he pops to his feet and disappears into the bush. There is no spoor, no hair, no blood, and no impala. He is gone! I am thinking to myself that I hope this nightmare ends soon as Nixon hands me a coke a cola.

He says, "Here Frank, drink this. Maybe you will wake up!"

I mutter back, "Aah things go better with coke."

Nixon tells me, maybe we need new bullets. We need soft points. And I think, "No shit Sherlock!" My response is that I need confidence in this gun. The only good thing that happened today is the last two times I had cleanly cleared the chamber and reloaded with the high throw bolt for the first times. I can't waste bullets practicing and besides right now the only difference between Nixon's and my own right shoulder is that his is all black and mine is black and blue. With hamburger for a shoulder and my confidence in the sewer, I am fighting myself to try to get my mind set to start shooting. I am battling a mental roadblock with this unfamiliar gun and mismatched ammo. I need to regain the

Frank Schmitz

force within me. To do so will take getting some confidence in this weapon.

Later that day we advance to a water hole lead by the Grim Reaper. At the edge of the swamp he says we must pick up sticks to carry with us, thus following the rules of an old native superstition. Nixon and I follow his lead and as we enter the swampy area the Grim Reaper says, "Throw down now and we will have luck!" We toss the sticks as we sneak into the marsh. We walk a short distance and spot a warthog rutting in the grass. Nixon and I stalk closer, looking, looking, no tusks. Then another one comes bursting into view from our left, a female; another young one; another young one; another; finally a big boar. The tusker breaks into the open charging across it towards the bush. There is no time to think, there are only seconds to react. As the gun floats to my shoulder, the scope to my eye, and my finger to the trigger - in an instant, a bullet is gone as the bolt in one fluid motion ejects the spent cartridge and chambers another. The second round is on its way. In the blink of an eye, without thought, the unconscious reaction sends 600 grains of lead pouring into the boar only inches apart. The first deflates his air bags and the second blows up his fuel pump. The force of the Jedi has returned, as the homely warthog lay dead. This time when my reactions had to be in split seconds, the unfamiliar gun became an extension of my heart, mind and soul - responding like poetry in motion. Maybe the witchcraft of carrying sticks is what I needed! Maybe I have overcome the black magic!

The INNER FORCE

Hunting here versus South Africa is significantly different. In South Africa it was much easier to see the game in the rolling and open spaces. That country meant that you had better be able to throw the long bomb. Here, where it is dense brush and flat, it is more conducive to the jump shooter. Several times en route to this area I had seen game standing and watching us as we drove by at 60 mph or so. In the bush when we come creeping along in the Land Rover they do not wait. Obviously they hear us and often wait to see what it is before fleeing. But when we spot them it is usually just fragments of an animal looking at us through the bush. One must identify the species, judge the caliber of the animal, aim and shoot all in a very short time span. It is proving to be extremely challenging, but if this gun becomes an extension of my arm, I will invariably put the shit to them.

This afternoon as we checked the leopard baits, we discovered a very big leopard had followed a dragline near the bait. He investigated it but failed to strike. Hopefully his stomach will convince him to do otherwise tonight. We spiced it up with some warthog meat and guts basted with giraffe stomach entails. How could anyone pass up a free meal of such fine delicacy!

After a big supper, we retired early. I believe I am beginning to develop a sleeping mood, as I crashed out like a "dead log." Perhaps the last episode of a clean kill has put my mind to rest.

Frank Schmitz

Its inspiring to watch the African trackers analyze soft prints in loose dire. These folks are not blinded in ability by merchandise and gimmicks like us Americans. They have to use their God given senses, judgment and instincts. They study spoor, sniff the air, feel the wind and listen to the bush. That is what gives the clues to where the game hides. They have no range finders, compasses or GPS's. They are unconcerned of their body odor because they know you have to play the wind. Their movements are fluid and quiet with ears tuned into their surroundings. They wear no camouflage because they understand the lack of importance it has. Their clothes are usually a drab green or tan and they wear baseball caps of any kind. This clothing is less to blend in but more to protect themselves from the bush and the sun- that is their important functions.

Unlike them we are prone to buy every gimmick imaginable. Not only do we pack high-powered rifles with scopes that have bullet drop compensators, light up cross hairs, so on and so forth; we also buy every other short-cut possible. Camo cloths, face masks, decoys, game calls, cover scents, game scents, range finders, G.P.S's, compasses, fancy boots, and tree stands. We bait, we gang up and push game, we use ATV's, we have motion cameras, and game timers, mock scrapes, and it goes on and on.

All short cuts to compensate for our lack of capability, our unwillingness to learn to hunt, blend in, to read the sign. What are the short cuts really worth? How do they reward the hunt? The real reward is to learn to hunt, blend in, beat the prey with its superior senses - to accept the fact that they will persevere almost every time. That is what creates trophy status. If it were easy there would be no challenge. If every N.F.L. team could win the super bowl every year, what would that honor be worth? Nothing!

The cool thing about hunting is you can set your own standards, make your own rules. Once you have achieved success at one level you can raise your own bar. Perhaps it would be better described as down shifting. Down shift - drop the rifle and pick up a bow or a muzzleloader. You can down shift again when harvesting becomes easy and let the animals walk. Set a goal and hold out for it.

Now you are hunting! That is how you get a trophy. The pinnacle of hunting is doing it your way, by fair choice, and by your standards. The higher your standards the tougher the hunt, the greater is the reward. Forget the gimmicks! You can buy gimmicks, just as you can buy game behind the fence, but what is it worth? Nothing!

In our mind all the gimmicks compensate for lack of ability. But in reality it handicaps us from learning our place in nature. Thus, making us less capable to become true woodsman.

My eyes are too heavy, I must sleep now because tomorrow surely will be a glorious day - as they all are in Africa.

Frank Schmitz

June 5

Today it is a little warmer than yesterday. I had the best and longest night's sleep in recent memory. My body felt totally relaxed and rested this morning and my muscles feel like they are ready for work.

Two species that are here, but that I haven't seen so far are the zebra and wildebeest. Both of which would be safe from my gun. I have seen many kudu but not a big one. If I do his fate would hang in the balance. They are like bull elk. Opportunity seldom knocks and when it does you had better appreciate it. The fate of the huge waterbuck that just stood before me on the first day as I passed him up would be different now. I have come to appreciate their tenacity and uniqueness. Opportunity may never come a knocking again, however. My main target animals, Cape buffalo and leopard, obviously are still just that. The beautiful sable appears to be rare, so it is unlikely that I will see one. Nixon told me I should just forget about it. Obviously, that species is not common to the area. The civet cat I saw yesterday would have been a beautiful trophy. It was black and white and sort of striped and spotted. It looked more like a mongoose than a cat. Very unordinary!

Well it is time for another cup of coffee before beginning the destiny of the day. We first checked leopard baits. No activity on this front. We have seen many giraffe and warthog this morning - as if they know I will not take them anymore. We also observed two bushbucks, one truly exceptional. They both just stood there and stood there. They are beautiful, like a kudu but much smaller. They also are not on the hit list and seemed to know it.

As we drove around I asked Nixon how the buffalo took his gun last year. He told me the hunter had wounded the buffalo and it had disappeared into thick cover. They entered the bush in search of it. Suddenly it comes from nowhere on a full charge. As the buffalo blasts past he tries to hook Nixon, tangling his gun strap on its horn. Nixon explained that this saved him because the buffalo thought it had him on his horn. It ran with the .416 tangled in his massive horns, smashing it into a tree. It broke the gun in two, thinking it had finished him. Meanwhile, Nixon runs and grabs the gun from the hunter and pounds him. Nixon finishes the bull instead of the other way around.

Frank Schmitz

One previous hunter was not as lucky. There is a grave marker at the entrance to camp. It is a rather nice head stone. It says, "In memory of Edward Dyckes," who was tragically killed near this spot by a buffalo on the 27th of January, 1955. That grave marker in camp keeps the reality of this hunt in perspective.

Later in the morning, we spot seven waterbuck; one big bull. They are 150 yards away and the bull is standing! A mere chip shot for the 7 mag. I draw a bead on him with the 375 H&H and fire. The 300 grain bullet punches a tiny one-quarter inch hole through the beast. It zips through, breaking nothing. The animal absorbs no energy, no percussion, it does not flinch and like the others, it runs off. We could not tell if the shot was high, low, left or right, but it was ineffective, leaving not a spec of blood. We decide not to push the waterbuck in hopes that he will stiffen up and remain close to the area. We will search for him tomorrow. The ineffective ammo betrays me again!

We had searched for a blood trail but found none. We did not want to push the animal, for they are strong and the bush is thick. It could easily cover several miles. He is lost and I say to Nixon, "That is it! I will shoot no more with this rifle and these useless bullets, far too much gun and bullet to be effective." My only choice is to trade up for yet an even bigger gun and bigger bullet.

Now, I am carrying another unfamiliar weapon, a .416 with 400-grain bullets. But at least the bullets are soft points and might do some damage. We will see. The bad part is we only have a dozen of these bullets left.

At least an arrow with a broad head would cut a hole one and one-half inches. A hole eight times larger than the hole the solid makes. The bullet is like shooting arrows with field tips on it, making a hole the diameter of the shaft.

As we set out this afternoon starting earlier than normal, I think to myself, this gun is unfamiliar. How does it shoot, what is the zero, the drop, etc.? I will be very conservative and only shoot if the animal is standing clear at 50 yards or less. In this country when game decides to have a look at you they stand in heavy cover peaking around a tree or something. I told myself, "Do not shoot unless the conditions are perfect." I did take one practice shot at fifty yards. The bullet hit three inches high and I suspected that would be about zero at one hundred yards.

Two hours later, we spot a herd of kudu - cow, cow, cow, cow, cow, calf, calf, cow, calf and then the biggest bull I have ever seen appears. They had heard us coming and were trotting away in very dense underbrush. We jump out of the Land Rover and follow them through several draws as they begin to distance themselves. It looks like we lost them but then there they are, off to our left. The pursuit continues.

The kudu is a large magnificent critter that weighs between 400 and 600 pounds. It's behavioral pattern reminds me of a whitetail deer. It is often referred to as the "Gray Ghost" because of its ability to disappear in a thicket, leaving neither hide nor hair of a clue to where he disappeared. Its size and grandeur remind me of an elk with its ability to show up or disappear at locations afar. The kudu is brownish-gray in color with thin white pin stripes decorating his backbone and sides. A distinct white chevron accents his forehead with long graceful spiraling horns adorning his crown. A kudu is the most majestic and royal looking ungulate on earth - in my book! A prized trophy indeed.

Frank Schmitz

I pressed somewhat hopelessly forward after the huge greater kudu the biggest one I had ever seen. I could not help but think of my first kudu. My first kudu rivals the trophy status of my first elk, my first whitetail and even my first small game trophy ever taken, a cottontail rabbit. What separates my first kudu from every other animal I ever hunted or killed is the shot. A shot that I expect will be my best shot ever.

On this day my guide, tracker, wife and I sat high on a mountainside watching what may or may not unfold below us. The evening before on a long shot, Tommy Couch had severely wounded an exceptional bushbuck. They lost it's track and were unable to recover it that night. This morning Tommy, his tracker and a parade of volunteers began to search out the valley below us. We decided to sit up high knowing that this could turn out to be one heck of a deer drive, if you will. All this activity could push a parade of game up this mountain valley. As the search moved forward to a big pond, which was the starting and finishing point of the recovery effort, we glassed below us. Nothing! Finally the search came to an end. This would be the only animal that Tommy and I would hit and not recover while collecting over thirty animals between us on that hunt.

We decided to proceed with whatever our next plan was to be and started towards the truck. At that moment John Bull chattered out in Africanize - Hogla Mjunga or something like that. We turned to look and below and across the canyon three kudu cows broke cover and ran for the top. Behind them followed a good kudu bull, the first I had ever seen.

Merrick glassed him and said, "To bad he is too far away, that's a nice bull." As I gazed upon the beautiful beast the inner force beckoned. "Do you mind if I try for him?" I asked.

With a rather astonishing expression Merrick answered "Well if you think you can make the shot!"

I brought my gun to bear, standing off-hand with out a rest, I took aim. I did not calculate yardage or windage but rather let the force within call upon my instincts. John Bull stood aside me with binoculars watching the event unfold. A flash of light came from my barrel as a tiny piece of lead blazed across the mountain at 3000 feet per second.

"Just over his back," John Bull announced as if to be a captain of a submarine watching a torpedo through his periscope that had been directed at an enemy ship. The Jeti-warrior in me calculated the next swipe of his sword as the muzzle flashed again. Bang the gun echoed across the canyon. Poowup, the distant sound of a hit echoed back. The cows turned directly up hill entering a heavy thicket with the bull behind them. Soon the cows exited the thicket near the crest of the mountain, disappearing over the top.

Frank Schmitz

The bull did not clear that thicket, except for his spirit which was departing his all too mortal body.

My P.H. Merrick was jumping up and down shouting "That is the best shot I have ever seen! That is undoubtedly the best shot, and off hand. I cannot believe it!"

I gazed down at the power of this piece of wood and steel in my hands, hardly realizing what I had just done. My first kudu ever, lay dead across a mountain, out of sight and in a small draw, no less than six hundred and fifty yards away.

That shot will probably stand as my best. Most folks should never think of trying a shot like that. As a matter of fact if you have to think about it you probably cannot make it and should not try. A kudu is a rather large animal and he was in a predominately open mountainside. A place where recovery of a wounded animal would be likely. I had been shooting out of my mind during the whole hunt, making instinctive reflex shots. When I asked if I could give it a try I wasn't wondering if I could make this shot. I knew I could! I'm not wanting to brag here, I am just stating the facts. When you're shooting instinctively your equipment has to be right on, but more importantly your mind has to be right on! When it's a reflex, it's like you can think your bullet to its target. It's a leap of faith - faith that comes from within. You just know when to pull the trigger - almost willing the bullet to the target. The only comparable shot I personally know of was a shot by Steve Boggs of California. He neck shot and killed a 6x6 bull elk across a mountain. The range finder verified it at 681 yards. Most animals being shot at that distance will stumble from wounds or be crippled - left to die a slow death elsewhere. If I would have had to consult with my P.H. on how high to hold, how far to lead - most likely I would have missed miserably.

That would have destroyed my confidence in my shooting ability, meaning that I would likely miss more often and be afraid to try good shots down the road. You have to build your confidence from close range working outward. You will know when a shot is ethical or not for you. A good rule of thumb is if you wonder if you can make the shot, don't try unless it's a paper target. Be a hunter - stalk closer and do it right.

For a second time, the kudu have vanished. All of a sudden I see them 100 yards ahead filtering through the brush at a trot. They slowly appear as they trot out of a brush-choked draw and then disappear over the top of the next ridge. I hurry ahead through

The INNER FORCE

the draw and onto the ridge. I waste no time as I rush along the ridge top looking for openings in the underbrush. I step out onto an old trail that offers an open shooting lane into the dense cover. At that moment a kudu cow trots into the lane, then another, and another. They are all going straight away as their flagged butts appear in the narrow channel between the underbrush.

Without realizing it when the big bull appears at the end of the string, the .416 is resting on my shoulder. The force apparently

Frank Schmitz

beckons as the canon thunders at the only shot available. Kaaaboom....thump! It disappears into the bush.

Bones says that I missed, but Nixon responds that he heard a hit. He asks, "Where did you aim?" I do not remember. I do not remember the gun coming up, the safety going off. All I know is one second I saw the bull entering the clearing and then he was in my scope. There was an explosion. I remember working the bolt, but the kudu were gone the next second.

We run to where they had been just moments earlier. There is a spec of blood and hair, so we start tracking specs of blood....a drop here, a drop there. The spoor is poor as we cover one hundred yards. Doubt clouds my mind and then the mighty kudu bull is standing before us swaggering like a town drunk, obviously fatally wounded. A quick shot sends him joyously off to the happy hunting grounds as wide grins grace the faces of the trackers. The Bwana redeems himself with high fives and hand shakes. The shot the blue-eyed one had instinctively taken is known as the Texas heart shot. The 400 grain bullet had entered four inches to the left of the bulls-eye and traveled through the kudu's entire body exiting just off center on the right front shoulder. How an animal could possibly absorb the shock of that guided missle ripping through the length of his entire body and not immediately crash to the ground I will never know. It is a very serious example of the shock resistance, stamina and strength of these African critters. They do not die easily. That is why many of these animals the ones that charge and bite back do so often.

It is time to rejoice as we stand over the beautiful creature. The kudu is one of the most common beasts of Africa, but widely respected as one of the toughest to kill. A big bull kudu is like an old whitetail buck. I marvel at the beast as I bend down to touch his massive spiraling horns, stained dark as black walnut - sweeping outward to ivory tips. I look at his thick, heavily maned neck and the distinct white chevron marking between his eyes - accented by his dark grey face and white muzzle. All this atop his slick gray muscular body pinstriped in dainty white lines. What a remarkable beast! Once you get Kudu fever it lasts forever....like those who are addicted to whitetail or elk in North America,

The INNER FORCE

I reflect how lucky I am to have my third kudu bull in only my second trip to Africa. In Ernest Hemingway's timeless classic "Green Hills of Africa" he and his companions struggled mightily to collect a kudu bull. Their hunt was sixty days long in 1932 in a virgin Africa, yet they struggled to harvest a kudu bull - becoming obsessed with trying to get one. Hemingway finally succeeded on the last day of that well documented trip. In his book he worried that places they hunted were already jeopardized by too much human encroachment and hunting. Carl E. Akeley's classic "In Brightest Africa" written in 1923 also expressed concern that Africa's game would soon follow the way of the American Bison and be exterminated. As he collected elephants to be mounted in museums in America, he was sure that they would become extinct in the next decades. Only memories would document the animals of wild Africa.

That was how rapidly our world was changing. In 1913, the year after Theodore Roosevelt finished his presidential term, he went on an Africa Safari that lasted over one year. He had an entourage of people, beasts of burden, and associates with him. Their objective was like Noah's except they did not intend to have animal's march two-by-two onto the Ark. Instead they intended to collect males and females of every species to be preserved at the Field Museum of Natural History in Chicago. That is where most

Frank Schmitz

of the beasts he collected reside to this day. They hired hundreds of porters, trackers, skinners and servants. They packed cases of ammo and four tons of salt for preserving skins as well as food, tents, clothing, booze and all other fineries royalty would need during a year in the bush. The cost of this expedition today would be about sixty million dollars. The exploits of this adventure were recorded in his book "African Game Trails," written shortly after the turn of the century. Africa was a travel destination for kings, aristocrats and royalty. But in the next ten years entrepreneurs realized they could slaughter elephants and rhinos for skins, tusks and horns, and turn huge profits. So the rape of the land began.

Fortunately for all these most splendid creatures of the earth the interior was deep. As the game was decimated in the outer edges the profitability subsided. I am sure that Roosevelt, Akeley and Hemingway would be mightily impressed if they were alive today to know that all the beasts of Africa have survived into the twenty-first century. And, that wild Africa still exists although only a fraction of its original glory. Still, Africa is substantially better off than our own glorious U.S. of A. If it was not for Roosevelt's great vision to establish Yellowstone and other parks our wild buffalo would be gone. It's too bad he didn't make all of Montana, Idaho and Wyoming part of Yellowstone National Park. Then we would really have something, wouldn't we?

Anyway, as long as there are places still wild and free for man to test himself against the forces of nature, the spirit of man can survive. If that is ever destroyed we will have destroyed ourselves; our spirit will die with the animals and earth will be a lonely place. Not because what is wild is lost, it will be what is free that is lost. The essence of the human race is freedom, just as it is the call of the wild. It is one in the same. We are them and, they are us - it is the common bond between man and beast. The reason to admire, desire, breed, proliferate, co-exist; to be born and die in the life and death cycle of eternal life - it is freedom for man and beast.

But it is time for celebrating as we load the big beast into the Land Rover and head for camp. We waste no time going to camp while the last light of the day is waning when a warthog jumps from the nearby bush. Nixon and I are in the bed of the truck as Nixon gives the traditional tap on its back window. This tap means stop - like right now!

The INNER FORCE

As the truck screeches to a halt, Nixon grabs the 416 and "kaaboom." The warthog tumbles over dead. I'm thinking, "I guess they are fond of pig and needed another for camp." I look at it and notice that it is severely injured with bullet wounds having torn open most of its right side. I realize this is the pig I had shot a couple days earlier. It was the one that got away. The first animal I had lost in Africa was just recovered. This critter could have been anywhere, but it just happened to be in the path we had chosen home. Unbelievable! How quickly things change. In spite of enormous obstacles to overcome with my weapons, at the end of the fifth day of hunting the fifth trophy animal lay on the ground. More importantly, recovering this wounded animal clears my state of mind. My confidence is rebuilding. Only in Africa could it be this way.

The greatest challenge lay ahead...The buffalo and leopard. If fate decides to present these challenges. It is becoming ever more unlikely that I will shoot at many more plains game. Ammunition is at a premium. We have nine rounds left for the .416. We know the twenty rounds of solids for the 375 are only going to be effective for crushing bone in a mammoth creature like the Cape buffalo. Tomorrow we will try to recover the waterbuck and check baits.

The native African culture is abnormal according to our belief since men can take as many wives as they like. It turns out Dixon (Bones) has two wives and eight children. On the other hand, Nixon has one wife and six children. Nixon is quite affluent and rules with an iron hand over his children. He has three boys whom all work with him in the safari business. Two of them are P.H.'s, which is a high status position. His three girls are still in school at the college level for Zimbabwe. He maintains tight control over them, even the twenty year old. She wanted to spend the night at a friend's house, but Nixon would not allow it. She was upset with him but he declared, "As long as you are in my house and I am paying for school, you will live by my rules." He is very careful to protect his children. They are not allowed to be sexually active until married....for good reasons.

AIDS originated in Zimbabwe and as the country became infected the rest of the world did not notice or care. People took notice once the disease spread outside of this region into the more developed world. What is this disease? Why are people dying? How is this spread? During the ten or more years of the virus' evolution, when it finally was identified and traced back, thousands of Zimbabweans had already died.

Forty percent of the population was infected by the time they started testing here. Thousands more will die, but you do not see it. Everyone looks healthy. Now that the people here understand the disease, they are being very cautious and are being tested before marriage. In spite of that, poverty stricken folks are promiscuous, spreading this virus. It makes you wonder which would be more life threatening; the mauling at the hand of a leopard or buffalo or the blood transfusions you would need to recover?

I am still beside myself that we recovered the wounded warthog. In a country that is this vast, almost endless, while littered with predators, that was unbelievable. My lucky horseshoe has regained its glow, so I sleep more easily then before. I believe we have a good chance of finding my water buck - time will tell. For now I had better try to sleep for the sand is filtering through my hourglass and soon it will be tomorrow.

June 6

Today was very cold in the morning, but clear skies warmed the earth quickly. We checked the leopard baits first and found no strikes. We then proceeded to where I shot the waterbuck yesterday. Waterbuck is an antelope of 400 pounds or so. They are tough and stout with long horns that curve slightly forward. Their most identifying marking is the white circle around their gray-brown tail end. It looks like someone drew a circle or a target on their butt.

We started to beat the bush hoping the waterbuck had not gone far, laid down and stiffened up. We were only one hour into the search when unbelievably the big old stag struggled to his feet 75 yards in front of me. This sight caught me off guard, as I really wondered if we would recover this magnificent beast.

Frank Schmitz

I hesitated thinking it might be another one but heard Nixon's command, "Shoot him Frank!"

I shouted back. "Is he the one?"

Nixon's quick reply was to trust him and shoot. I knew that his keen instinct would easily decipher a wounded animal from a healthy one. Nixon is the man. Nixon for president! The .416 came to bear bare and in an instant the 400-grain slug was on its way. The soft point crumbled him like a sand castle in a hurricane. Yippie-ky-yaah. The sweet taste of victory is mine and I have now exorcized all my demons. Unbelievably, with all the problems I was having with these weapons, we now have recovered all the

The INNER FORCE

wounded game. My confidence is soaring with the .416 and I believe I have found the force within! Life is good!

The waterbuck bull is a huge one. His horns are thick and long. His body muscular and massive. This is a beast I had not intended to hunt, but a wonderful trophy. Nixon grasps my hand and holds it tightly as he rejoices with me. Holding hands is a sign of friendship, trust, and an expression of happiness in Africa. They are not insecure, like we Americans who are afraid to show emotion.

We rejoice over recovering this magnificent creature. His long ribbed horns sweep upwards hooking forward at the top. His eyes are accented with a white mask and his coat is a slick tawny brown with the traditional white circle around his posterior. His scent is strong and sweet like that of a horse, and for a moment I miss my four legged friends back home. AHHH, today is a great day - a day to remember!

It is important that people understand the significant need for hunting in Africa, and anywhere as far as that goes. As long as there is hunting these animals will flourish. If the hunting stops then the animals are doomed. The reason is pure and simple economics. As long as the game has market value, people will allow the wild game to compete on the land with their livestock. If the game were to have no value, the locals will trap and snare them until they are gone. If the only animals left on earth live in parks and refuges where people go to photograph and feed them, then the wildlife is gone. If these animals no longer fear man they have lost what they are. If they begin to rely on man for handouts like the bears once did in Yellowstone, we have robbed them of their freedom and stolen their survival instincts. Then they are cows and pigs to be raised for slaughter or entertainment like a dog or cat. They are no longer wild and free.

Today in Zim there are 88,000 elephants. Twenty-five years ago there were only 10,000. The return of the elephant is great, but the problem is the parks and wild habitat can only support 45,000 elephants. Right now the locals are deforesting the land which threatens to annihilate other species as well as themselves. There is no place to go with the elephants. There are simply too many. The rest of the world bans ivory importation so people won't kill elephants. These people are poor. The fair market value of an elephant with its tusks and high quality leather is very high. These people could desperately use the income. They would

Frank Schmitz

like to utilize these animals because of the need to kill them to save the forests and parks. The elephants will probably go to waste because our society will not accept the truth.

I have had many people ask me why I hunt. How could you kill these animals? Let me try to explain. As mentioned before, we are part of the life and death cycle. It is Mother Nature's way. We come from the dirt, are sustained by the dirt, and will return to the dirt. The cycle never stops. We must kill to survive. One thing dies to sustain the other! It does not matter if we kill plant life or animal life or both to sustain ourselves. Our impact on the earth

The INNER FORCE

and environment is the same. The vegetarians create demand to destroy the forest and its wildlife to plant crops. Their hands are equally as bloody as the meat eaters. The cycle is eternal.

There are predators and there are prey. Anything that lives by breathing oxygen is a predator. Anything that lives by breathing carbon dioxide is prey. It is all sustained by air and water. If you breathe oxygen you are a predator and kill either plant or animal life or both to survive. Humans are predators. Bambi is a predator. A beetle or an ant is a predator. They all survive by seeking prey to sustain themselves. They all hunt. Some to kill plant life, others to kill animal life.

If you believe in the greater power, then you should believe in the word of God. In the creation story in the book of Genesis the word of God reads as he gave the first people his orders: "Be fruitful and multiply and replenish the earth and subdue it and have domain over the fish of the sea and over the fowl of the air and over every living thing that moveth upon the earth." In Genesis 9:2-3 it states, "The fear of you and the dread of you shall be upon every beast of the earth and upon every bird of the air, upon everything that creeps on the ground and all the fish of the seas, into your hands they are delivered. Every moving thing that lives shall be food for you and as I give the green plants, I give you everything".

That was the word of God. If you don't believe there is a God, if you believe you are just here through evolution and when you die, you die, then you are particularly blind to reality and certainly in a state of denial. The earth promises eternity, a concept that should be easy to grasp and understand. If you look into the sky with the most powerful telescopes known to man the heavens go on indefinitely....more suns, more planets, more universes. Eternity is all around us. Dead matter goes into the soil, into the plant, into the animal and back into the soil. It never stops, never has, never will. It will go on forever.

So why should a hunter have to justify he is responsible for his own existence, that he accepts reality. I think the ones who deny who and what they are; deny eternity; deny the fact that they are part of the life cycle; and, deny that they are responsible for their own impact on the environment should explain to me! Tell me why they pay others to kill for them; to plow the fields, destroy the land, and pave it over to build schools for their children and homes and so on and on... Tell me Judas , I am listening!

Frank Schmitz

    I decided to sit on the sandy sunny beach of the river that meandered in front of camp to write in this journal. I had been there about an hour and gotten up to walk to my quarters when, turning around and looking back to the beach where I had just been minutes ago, I could not believe my eyes. Standing precisely where I had been sitting stood a big male baboon. It was obvious that he and his tribe had patiently been watching and studying me. As soon as I left, the dominant male went to investigate the area. You can only wonder how smart they really are.

The INNER FORCE

Things never do not ever get boring in the bush because it is constantly evolving. As Mother Nature plays her game, new cards continually fall on the table. We discovered that as we slept last night, just a short distance from where I scribbled this babble on paper, a leopard had killed a bushbuck. Almost right in camp! It apparently wanted to remove the kill from such close proximity to the camp and had dragged it hundreds of yards down river. From there it dragged it across the water into a stand of swamp grass. The grass was eight feet tall so we could not find any volunteers to go into the grass and take a look around. I guess nobody is ready to meet their maker yet!

We set several more baits in new locations with scraps of guts from the waterbuck. It is surely only a matter of time until a leopard will strike. We spotted a good impala. Nixon advised I take him, but I stated I would shoot no more unless we are successful at the Cape buffalo and leopard. We are very low on ammunition for the .416.

I found the remains of some baboons in an abandoned water tank. The tank had concrete walls seven, maybe eight feet high and is about thirty feet across with a dry concrete floor. They apparently had fallen in and could not escape. I collected several skulls from the tank. At one point, I considered shooting one of those hideous bastards, but now have grown fond of them as they watch and interact with me at camp.

Impressive animals grace the landscape of Africa - there are so many. The magnificent cats; lion, leopard and cheetah; the hideous hyena; the one of a kind giraffe; the prehistoric elephant and hippo; rhino and cape buffalo. Then there are gorillas and 20 feet crocodiles. Often overlooked is the endless array of spectacular antelope, kudu, sable, wildebeest, gemsbok and the rare bongo.

With all that, there is one beast that often gets overlooked, but shouldn't. It is a hoofed animal that can leap a seven foot fence. It weighs in at or near a ton. Not only is the finest table fare in Africa, but to my knowledge, the best eating wild game on the face of the earth. This animal is the Eland! A stout critter that looks more like an oxen with his long floppy dewlap. However it has a handsome face with twisting, straight horns protruding from his head.

Frank Schmitz

On a previous Safari, I had a veteran safari hunter warn me that I didn't have enough gun to hunt eland. He had a night-marrish experience with an eland - repeatedly shooting one while pursuing it over a mile before subduing the might beast. When he was done the hunter had torched sixteen rounds through the barrel of his 375 H&H. Obviously he had not put on a shooting clinic, but he figured I was way under-gunned with a 338.

Our trackers reported finding a pair of eland tracks heading across the open plains to a lone mountainous ridge. I took the biggest gun I had with me, the 338 A-bolt. Our plan was for me to travel around the mile long ridge one way while the trackers went the other. We hoped the eland would hold to the brushy cover on the ridge forcing them towards me, or that I would come unto them. I hunted to the end of the ridge on my side of the mountain without an incident. Upon reaching the end of the ridge I decided to sit down and wait for the trackers coming from the opposite side, hoping that they may be pushing game ahead of them.

Terri accompanied me as we sat waiting. We were entertained by watching a herd of twenty black wildebeest frolic around out on the open plains. These beasts are called the clowns of Africa and are comical to observe. They prance and bounce around in animated unnatural movement. They act as if they are dancing on hot coals while being attacked by a swarm of killer bees. Soon the big top carnival act was interrupted by the sound of hooves against hard ground coming our way. Then there was movement in the bush as a herd of Zebras came trotting by from the opposite ridge. This was just another awe inspiring scene as the zebras trotted down to join the clowns of Africa. Ringling Brothers would be hard pressed to upstage this show.

When we thought it could not get any better the sound of animals on the move regained our attention. More hooves beat the ground coming from where the zebras had recently passed. Again we strained our eyes into the bush as springbuck appeared. Lot's of springbuck! Perhaps thirty head trotted by on the dry, African soil sending up a cloud of dust ten feet into the sky. They kept appearing one by one out of the smoke screen their movement created.

Suddenly, two ghostly shadows of enormous proportions began to emerge from the clouds of dust.

The INNER FORCE

Their silhouettes slowly materialized into sold forms. They dwarfed the tiny springbucks with their grandeur and hulking mass. It was the pair of eland we had sought. I drew a bead on the big bull wondering if my 338 was up to the mission at hand. He was passing our position at 150 yards when my 225-grain nozler bit him in his front shoulder. He absorbed the impact without flinching - like the mighty oak tree he was. My second shot directed at the same place hit him with the force of Paul Bunyan's mythical ax, splitting his hardwood trunk and rolling him to the ground. With the grace of an acrobat he rolled completely over and right back onto his feet. Now, standing in defiance of his attack, the third shot blasted again into his massive front shoulders. This time Paul Bunyan's ax shattered the mighty oak, turning him into kindling. The biggest beast I had ever hunted now lay lifeless in front of me. Soon we were met by the trackers and rejoiced, but not too much because a big job now lay in front of us. Latter that night we cooked eland back straps on an open fire, steaks so tender we could cut them with a fork. Ahh, the beauty of Africa. She is so marvelous at times, but she is two faced and one never knows when she will raise her ugly head - the dark side of the Dark Continent.

Late this afternoon, I went back to the river and sat there. Almost instantly I could hear the apes call to me. A screaming call that sounds threatening. After a half-hour they came to the opposite shore to investigate me. Later they crossed the river to my side. I am sure they came to the spot to see what I was doing after I left. I placed candy on the log where I sat and will see tomorrow if they took it.

The INNER FORCE

We discuss plans for the hunt. We only have the dangerous game left - cape buffalo, leopard and crocodile. With at least eight baits now set somewhere (some at the park) we can only wait for a strike. Meanwhile, unless there is a strike in the morning, we will travel three hours to the Chipimbi River Camp to begin buffalo hunting.

Frank Schmitz

June 7

Yesterday morning was perhaps the coldest to date, but the skies were clear and it got hot out. This morning it is the warmest so far, but the skies are cloudy and overcast. I slept poorly last night lying awake from 1:30 AM until morning. I was thinking of my wife, again feeling very alone. This is the midway point of my hunt so I had better keep my mind on the business at hand. I mean hunting. I heard the baboons calling from outside my room at 4:30 AM or so. Maybe they want more candy.

Today we travel to the Chipimbi River to an area that Nixon had his son, Simon, scouting for buffalo. He located them the day before yesterday and summoned us here to give chase.

Just when I thought I knew what was next, one of the locals reported a twelve-foot crocodile on the lakefront by our camp. Being the dry season the lake has receded substantially, maybe fifty percent, leaving long mud banks. The crocs like to sun themselves on this dark mud seeing as they are a cold blooded creature. To kill a crocodile can be a challenge. The best shot is a brain shot between the eyes. However, his brain is very small, so the shot must be accurate. If a side shot presents itself, you go for the neck at the base of the skull. The same from behind.

When we got to the shore the croc had already slipped back in the water and was gone. A blind was quickly erected - sticks for a frame with leaves and branches woven in and out of the frame to create a three-sided blind. Two holes about the size of our faces were left open in the front to view and shoot through. Then Nixon, Bones and I sat in the blind and waited. I could see crocs surface and slowly, very slowly, drift back and forth in the lake. On the surface of the water their exposed heads looked like thin horizontal lines. I could not believe how much this resembled an African hunting computer game I have to a tee. Even the sound of the bush was identical to the game. On the game as you hunt different animals, you run the risk of being charged or attacked. When this happens, you try to shoot the attacking critter before it kills you, 'ending' the game. Well, about four out of the ten times I first played the game, I would shoot at the croc and it would attack and eat me. In the real world, crocs do not kill many people, mostly native folk when they go to the river for water.

Frank Schmitz

Well, we sat there and watched. It reminded me of duck hunting on a day when no birds were flying. Sit and wait - a boring game. It is like watching paint dry. Not really. I did see bushbuck come to the waters edge and risk a drink. After a couple hours we saw the big croc edging up on the shore 500 yards away. Nixon figured he smelled us or just knew we were there. I guess they do not live for 100 years because they are stupid.

It is mid-morning. I have just eaten a lunch of spaghetti and beef, bread, cheese and beans. As I ate I thought about how many hunters have been killed by Cape buffalo. There is a chance, a very real chance that I am eating my last meal. I am glad that I have Nixon for a P.H. He is professional, experienced, a marksman and does not take foolish chances. He knows this is a high stakes game we are playing.

Nixon showed off his skill with a rifle last night when he shot an impala for some tribesmen. The fact that he killed the impala which was only forty yards away was not impressive, even if they are rather small and where in thick cover. They were just walking and stopping and so forth. The impressive part was he lined them up and took two with one shot! Nixon understands this game. He knows how these animals think. That is why we recovered the warthog and waterbuck.

I had vervet monkeys outside my door a few minutes ago playing peek-a-boo. I do not know what they tried to tell me. All I know is very soon I will be buffalo hunting. I hope they were wishing me luck - not wanting to see me for the last time!

With a couple hours before high noon, we hurried off to the area where buffalo had been sighted grazing earlier. The damned buffalo are the size of pickup trucks and the herd was reported to have up to one hundred in it. You would think it would be easy to relocate a herd of animals bigger than a new car lot in the bush. You would think. We drove to the area and searched it back and forth, wherever we could get with the Land Rover. Nixon commented with a frustrated frown on his face, "Where did they go? I do not get it. They cannot disappear. These are big animals. Only place can be down through the draw."

Actually the brush is very, very dense with a good shot being fifty yards. Buffalo could hide anywhere and everywhere, but a whole herd makes noise and dust. It should show up.

Nixon, Dixon and I start hiking into the bush along with the natives whom had spotted them earlier. We go up and down through drainages, across openings and in and out of dense brush for an hour — nothing. We start through the bush towards the truck and all of a sudden everything starts rumbling; black movement, snapping twigs, breaking branches, you can feel the ground tremble and there are low grunting sounds. I push the safety off on the .416 as the bush stirs around us with the buffalos circling toward the left. I can see black silhouettes in the bush, some pausing to look at us. They stampede off and we follow. We walk fast. We trot. We walk. We run. We trot. We do whatever it takes to try and stay close. The buffalos move off and stop in thick brush until they see us and stampede off again.

When we close in they watch from the dense brush, well concealed and run off again. At one point I could see a big buffalo standing and staring at me. Looking at it head-on at seventy-five yards I could not believe how broad its shoulders were. It looked a good four feet across its back! I quickly realized why I had a .416 in my hands.

Frank Schmitz

Actually, I wondered why I did not have a 600-nitro express with heat seeking missiles armed with small nuclear warheads in my grasp! They looked like big bears, just black blobs. I couldn't see their shoulders or necks, so I would have to draw a mental picture when taking aim to shoot. Nixon is armed with the 375 for backup and that is a comforting thought. The buffalo turns. The ground rumbles. Brush cracks and snaps and they are gone. We are off trotting again in pursuit as I wonder how long we have to do this in order to get them to stand; or how long we have to do

The INNER FORCE

this before we initiate a charge. If that happens it's going to be close and fast and in this thick cover - it will be exciting!

Early this afternoon we relocated the buffalo and continued the cat and mouse game. They gave us the slip and we spent a couple hours trying to catch back up with them by foot. At one point, I got this twitch in the pit of my stomach and a tingle going down my spine. I hadn't heard, seen or smelled anything, but I knew something was about to happen. I'm sure you have had that feeling that someone is watching you, but when it happens here you immediately start checking your back track! You just don't know for sure! A minute later the earth started to rumble, brush breaking. Buffalo, they sure can't sneak away from you. Later in the day we split up to confuse and/or separate the buffalo.

At one point, I heard the thunder of hooves coming right at me through the bush! I wondered if I was going to get run over, but a disadvantageous breeze lifted my scent to the buffaloes' noses. They turned and barreled like a runaway timber wagon down the hill. Every incident is exciting with these critters that could stamp our frail ass into the earth!

By mid-afternoon they had outdistanced us so we relinquished pursuit to rest a couple hours. The sun is high and warm, the ground dry and dusty. All the creatures rest and conserve energy at midday. So do we. I close my eyes and see the big black beasts dancing in my mind, their shadowy silhouettes blending into the shade of the underbrush. The element of danger pumps adrenaline through my veins, electro charging life itself. The game of man and beast, life and death is definitely electrifying. Sometimes we get caught up in the routine of life. Then our lives are just a series of motions. We are living but not alive, just passing time to get to the world after! When you hunt buffalo you are alive. Each moment is excitement. It is true adventure!. The age old struggle of life and death is a game of fulfilling life itself, of being alive and there are no winners or losers, just a continuation of the life cycle as man or beast ultimately transcends to the next level, the world after!

Africa always challenges your life or well being. Although I escaped the plague of many of the poisonous vermin of Africa, I did not get out of the country without contracting a disease. I ended up with Recetsial Coroni, a sickness that can hospitalize you rather quickly. It is contracted by tick bites. After I was in Zimbabwe for three days with my P.H. and tracker, they showed

Frank Schmitz

me ticks that were on them. The ticks were as tiny as a pinhead and very hard to see. The locals would go through great pains to brush them from their legs and arms. I thought they were some sort of a gnat and they just called them ticks. I did not think they were ticks in the form of North American ticks. After all, the animals we harvested had ticks on them that were similar in size and conformation to our ticks.

We got into the ticks by the hundreds on days seven through ten of the hunt. Often we would have a hundred on one leg at a time! I did not even notice them biting me. I just brushed them off like my comrades were doing. On day ten, I realized these little buggers were blood sucking ticks when I noticed several buried into the inside of my arm by my elbow. They were enlarged from drinking my blood. I picked them off, not giving them a second thought. I also had some bothersome bites on my right ankle, the left side of neck and on my upper thigh. They seemed to act like spider bites.

I was homeward bound before I learned the side effects of Recetsial Coroni, also known as African Tick Bite Fever. Only one in a thousand ticks generally is a carrier of this virus. When they bite they infect your blood stream with a microbial invader. The microbes spread though your body causing a high fever that can easily render you bed ridden for days. I do not know how far it can go untreated. I do know that it will, if untreated for days like mine was, cause all the other tick bites to react.

The bites bubble up into puss heads similar to measles or chicken pox. That is why I know I was bitten 167 times on my right ankle; 98 times on my left ankle; 212 times on my legs, butt and chest; and 47 times on my arms. I had more spots than a leopard. Three spots were infected with the dominant sore located on my right ankle. This spot turned black and blue. It grew to the size of a silver dollar with a quarter inch black scab in the center that was highly infected with the larvae of some damn bug! I broke it open and poured hydrogen peroxide in the wound and swabbed the bites until I got antibiotics to fight the invader from my system. Several nights I broke into such intense fevers that my pillow and sheets would be drenched. If I got up from bed my silhouette would be easily visible in the wringing wet sheets. The infected bite areas take one to two years to heal and often scars for life – so another body tattoo! I carry several scars, distorted

The INNER FORCE

fingers and so forth; all a reflection of my reckless adventurous life. The prices you pay for discovery and adventure!

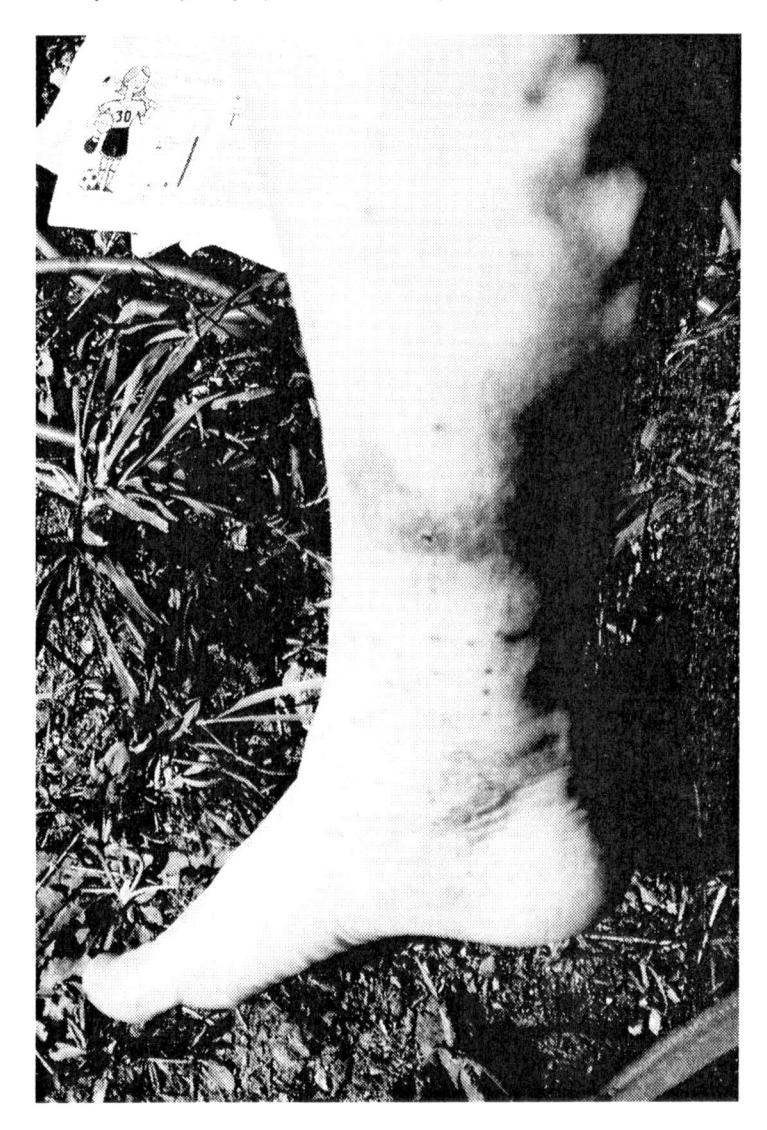

I previously stated how you cannot go to Africa only once. That it gets in your blood and keeps calling you back! Yet you have to be careful because there is a dark side.

This is probably the understatement of the century. Because when it gets in your blood it can overcome you. The dark side can come calling and it might have your number. You might not

Frank Schmitz

be in the yellow pages, your number even may be unlisted, but she will find you. Like a cheating husband trying to cover-up a one-night stand, you can run but you cannot hide from the kiss of this strange land. She is with you, in your blood! That is what happened to me. Fourteen months after supposedly beating my bout with Recetsial Coroni, the micro invader in my blood stream caused my left ankle to swell up.

I was building a spike camp in the backcountry for elk hunting when I began to turn lame. Within days my right foot started to swell as blood veins ruptured in my feet. Within a week I was disabled and could not stand up. The excruciating pain in my ankles and feet made it feel like I was walking on a bed of hot coals. My ankles continued to swell, turning black and blue as the local doctors tried to analyze the problem. I spent four days with my feet elevated, fighting the burning pain. The doctors thought it was a circulation problem and then, two weeks into it I came down with a bad sinus infection.

I was determined to carry on with my guiding duties so we packed up horses with gear, food and hunter's to ride into camp. My sinuses were draining and I thought the infection was finally clearing up. The next morning I awoke in camp with a severely restricted chest. Now I could hardly breathe as well as hobbled with sore feet. I realized that I could not carry on as the hunters left camp with my guide Quirt. That morning I hiked the five miles out of camp to go revisit the doc. The mysterious ailment continued even after another week of taking antibiotics and blood thinner for circulation.

Soon a month passed with all test's turning out negative. There were no answers to the ailment. Hot spots continued developing in my legs and feet while the lung infection now left me breathless. Climbing the stairs to my all too familiar bed left me gasping for air, while my feet burned and pounded with pain.

A thousand mile's away one of my first hunters consulted with his doctor on my condition. For this I am indebted to a fine, concerned human being. Thank you Don Gard! Analyzing the information, his doc said it sounded like a fungus infection similar to jungle boot rot our G.I.s contracted in the Vietnam War. With this background and more information from the 21st century Internet, we realized this fungus infection could be causing the disabling foot infections and could have spread through my body into my lungs. A fatal infection if not treated.

The INNER FORCE

By now I was six weeks into this downhill battle before I could see an infectious disease specialist. My only treatment was taking painkillers and applying anti-fungal ointments on my legs and feet. I felt like a worn out old horse that needed to be put down as we entered our busy fall hunting season. Unable to hike, hunt or guide, Terri and I traveled 4 hours to see the specialist. I had been hampered by broken bones, torn muscles and allergy ailment many times before, but never have I been so disabled like this.

The doctor quickly diagnosed the fungal infection and the lung infection. Medication was administered to fight off both of them. The first night after treatment my legs cracked with unbearable agonizing pain. Pain so intense I could not lie down or sleep. I spent the night coughing and stumbling around our lodge sleepless trying to deal with the pain. The very next night I slept like a "dead log" without any pain. I finally was on the right road - the road to recovery. Although it would be weeks before I could wear shoes and months to recover fully. At least we had treatment.

(Although this was what I believed to be the case as I wrote this book. The story takes another dreaded and morbid twist. Like a news report from Paul Harvey - check for additional information at the end of the book "for the rest of the story.")

We will never know if this was a haunting return of the dark side of Mother Nature's attempt to subdue me from Africa or a strange twist of fate of some other cause. Hopefully these ailments have not taken too big of a toll, because this earth with its pitfalls still does not outweigh its peaks. I would like to grace its wondrous surface for a long time to come. One needs to suffer through low's in order to really appreciate and enjoy the highs!

The tick bite fever was the sickest I have ever been from insect bites, but it was not my first run in with bugs! As a child I was infatuated with the outdoors and started collecting bugs, butterflies, moths and bees! My mother and father claim that I would catch bees by their wings as they pollinated flowers. I do remember having dozens of bumblebees, honeybees, wasps and hornets in Skippy peanut butter jars. These captured bees were obviously unhappy as I transferred pint jars of captured bees into one-gallon pickle jars. I remember fumbling around with several jars and dropping the lids as the mad insects escaped, surrounding me in my parents' garage. I slowly walked out without being stung!

Frank Schmitz

My running buddy, Rick Thome, and I would stir up a bumblebees' nest in his dad's barn and then quickly climb into the attic to hide from the mad bees. One day a bee got under my shirt as I climbed the ladder to supposed safety. It proceeded to sting me nine times on my back while I tried to squash the little bugger. My sister, Ann, freaked out and ran home like a rabid hyena screaming bloody murder. When my mom finally settled her down to see how she got mortally wounded, she gasped out between tears, "The bees are biting Frank!" Mom was relieved to see she was okay, but surely wondered what was coming next.

Years later I was working in Texas when my Siberian husky, Tobuck, started throwing a fit near midnight. In a pair of shorts and barefooted, I walked out to check on him. As I petted him trying to calm him down and figure out what the problem was, I realized that something was crawling up my legs. Hundreds of somethings! I reached down to brush off my legs and then the stinging bites started. I was knee deep in fire ants. Each bite was a little tiny cigarette burn. I jumped into Tobuck's five-gallon bucket of water while I struggled to unleash my faithful friend. We both ran for the house while swatting and brushing our legs and feet. I ended up with sixty-seven bites, mostly on my feet. They took months to heal up. Yes, fire ants sucked, but not as bad as love bugs!

My daughter, Sara, proved to be a good athlete and outdoors woman at a young age. By the time she graduated from high school, she had already harvested a couple of whitetail as well as a black bear. As a reward for being on the honor roll, I took her alligator hunting in Louisiana. Hunting alligators is sort of like fishing. We would paddle our way through marshes in a pirogue (a small shallow skiff-like boat) while setting baits. Each bait was a combination of 100 feet of 200-pound test line attached to a six-inch shark hook. One end was tied to bundled up swamp grass or a tree and the other suspended above the water by a forked branch. On the shark hook hung a quarter of a chicken and a chunk of beef liver.

The INNER FORCE

At night the prehistoric reptiles would swim along at the surface in search of prey. When they smelled our bait, they would close in on it, leap from the water and grab it. The next day we would come back to check the baits. If there was a hit, we'd go to where the line was tied off and start a hand over hand retrieve until the battling gator appeared from the murky depths. At that point the only way to subdue the nasty dinosaur would be to cap him in the brain bucket with my 375 hand gun.

It would get exciting at times, but never more exciting than when the line was in the swamp grass on shore rather than in the swampy water. Then your only choice would be to follow the line into the tall grass where an alligator can outrun a man for at least the first thirty-five feet. The problem is that the alligator would not be in the mood to run away from you, but rather right at you! To compound this adventure, I was hunting with one leg in a cast seeing as I broke it several weeks before the trip.

We did have one alligator charge us. Luckily I was able to direct my slug into his one-inch brain before I would have had to resort to sticking my cast in his mouth to slow down the toothy charge! Several weeks latter I reported to my doctor's office to have the cast removed from my leg. Sand began to pour out of the cast as if it was an hour glass when the doc's assistant sawed the cast in half. He inquired, "What the heck! Where the heck did

Frank Schmitz

the sand come from?" I replied innocently, " I don't know." Then as he split the cast open, low and behold there was a brilliant green piece of seaweed about 8 inches long, doing quite well in the moist cast. The puzzled assistant looked at me - apparently afraid to ask.

We took sixteen gators up to ten feet in three days. Successful by any measure, but the part that stuck in my mind more than the gruesome reptiles is the inch long ant-like flying love bugs.

One day our guide, Gene, and I slowly poled our way in our little skiff through a flat open marsh as we headed towards camp. We were happier than a couple of dead pigs in the sunshine, seeing as we had harvested four gators that morning. Our only fear was that we may be knocked out of the little boat by a twitching tail as the dead gators' reflexes stayed active for hours.

We worked our way homeward, sitting in the pirogue with gators lying on each side of us when suddenly a cloud of bugs appeared. Thousands of the flying love bugs swarmed down upon us in search of solid ground to carry out their breeding activities. With no place to go we were engulfed by the white winged creatures. Literally hundreds of them took refuge on each of us!

The iNNER FORCE

I would look down at my arms just coated with bugs and gently wipe them off as dozens crawled over my face. Then I would wipe my face while dozens more recoated my arms. You could not talk or open your mouth unless you wanted to devour the pests. For an hour I brushed the bugs simultaneously from my arms and face as we moved forward in the swamp. It was maddening. It was Chinese torture, making one want to dive into the swamp to escape. I struggled with myself to maintain mind over matter so as not to go crazy. We finally edged into brush country giving the critters something else that was stationary to sit on. Eventually they all opted for the brush and our sanity returned!

Now back in Africa, we play cat and mouse with the buffalo until it is dark. It is an exciting game - the buffalo won today. We drive back to camp in the darkness of Mother Africa as yet another great day has come to an end. If you get bored in Africa there is nothing left in life to excite you. You then must be the living, walking, dead.

It makes me realize what a challenging trophy a wild elk is. Even in my elk camp where we have a good population, it is not uncommon to hunt all week and not see one. A person can expect to hunt two years to take a bull and only take a true trophy occasionally. Although the game abounds here, our goal is to harvest mature animals, not super trophies by record book standards. I am a master measurer for Safari Club International. To get caught up in killing record book animals is an unhealthy situation.

Record books (be it SCI, Rowland & Ward, Boone and Crocket or Poe & Young) all serve a purpose and can give recognition to a lucky or skilled hunter. Most of all if you understand an animal's score, it gives us a good means of judging and communicating the size of an animal's horns or antlers. For instance, if I say that I saw a nice three-point buck, what kind of a mental picture do you visualize? In places out West, people only count the points of one side, so it could be a six pointer by Eastern count. Yet in other places they don't count the brow tine or eye-guard. Is it now an eight pointer? Eight points come in tiny little basket racks quite often - so what did I see? If I say I saw a 195 class eight point, anyone understanding scoring knows that it is a whopper for an eight point!

This is where the scoring system really helps hunting. But when people go to extremes to kill a record book animal - that is

Frank Schmitz

when it gets bad. People will poach, sneak in parks, hunt at night and do other illegal tactics trying to get a record book animal. They are not hunters or sportsmen. They are scum. It is often the books bring out the worst in some people.

"Killing" becomes so important over "hunting" that it has fueled a whole new industry in the U.S. and Canada...game farms - where people go to shoot pre-scored farm-raised deer and elk. This is evolution at the bottom of the barrel. I have read articles where outdoor writers endorse these places and pretend they are hunting - anything for a free hunt and story. Animals often are rounded up; the antlers are scored and/or inserted with copper so abnormal points and drop tines form; and then force-fed high protein food and steroids to ensure they grow an abnormally large rack. Any writer who pretends farm deer and elk eating on manipulated feed and steroids with sometimes manipulated antlers is like hunting wild game is or never was a hunter! They probably have a financial interest in the shooting preserve, too.

I have been on game farms and they are fun if you take it for what it is. It is nice that exotic game can be offered to the general public, most of who will never afford the opportunity to hunt abroad. Also, the ranches have saved some species from near extinction, reintroducing them into the wild. The black buck antelope, one of the beauties of the world, cannot be hunted in its native land. Instead it is being reintroduced from game farms to reestablish a wild herd. This activity may have saved the species and its gene pool.

I have had fun on game farms and it can be challenging going for animals that maintain good wild instincts. I once pursued a particular aoudad on a preserve for three days before I saw him. But I knew from the first minute to the last that I was going to find him eventually. It was entertaining, challenging and fun. But it was not hunting by the standards of fair chase by any means. Game farms have a purpose to entertain and save gene pools of rare species, but native game does not fall into this category. Raising and manipulating native game devalues the status of the species, devalues its trophy status and respect while jeopardizing its health and natural resilience to disease.

There is something drastically wrong when we capture and pen raise our wild animals, robbing them of their instincts, their dignity, and their natural ways. To force feed and manipulate them solely to kill them for their large racks or antlers is misguided. All

The INNER FORCE

to pacify some inner human desire so that we can say we killed an animal that possesses a record book type of rack. This entire concept is fueled by pure greed and money. In these penned places people pretend to outfit and guide others, while others pretend to hunt. At the end of the day a domesticated animal that relied on our hands to be fed lies dead while we pretend to have accomplished something. His sorry head is destined for some pathetic wall of fame or shame. These places are built on pure greed and a reflection of our darker side. It is sick and a far greater threat to hunting than the anti-hunter factions.

Raising wild game, unnaturally feeding it, manipulating it all should be stopped. Safari Club International, the world leader in promoting good wildlife policies, should get off their butts and lead the way instead of promoting this. I listened to the great General Schwarzkopf speak at a national convention for SCI several years ago. He supports the organization whole heartedly, but said to be leaders you need to clean up the ranks. I think this is what he was referring to. It is time to stand tall!

There usually is a high price to be paid when man plays with Mother Nature. These artificially enhanced animals' immune systems are jeopardized. They will not be resilient to disease, spreading it rapidly. Disease passed to wild herds will cost everyone dearly. All because a few greedy people whom could not hunt or be satisfied with a trophy wild animal for what it was, created a demand to buy these drones. These game animals have been robbed of their freedom, domesticated and raised for slaughter. The men who shoot them should be proud of the beautiful displays they make, but the mounts are no more a trophy on an office wall than is the door to enter the office. They are merely an image of what is wild and free just as the person behind the desk is merely image of a man. His balls are nothing but a mud flap for his vagina and it would be no different if the person was a woman pretending to have a mud flap.

I know all this because I have been there and done that! I have never stooped so low as to dishonor native game and shoot it behind the fence. But I have hunted behind the fence and am not ashamed of the critters I killed. I hunted in a one mile by one-mile enclosure in Texas with my good friend Tommy Couch of Sanderson. We knew there were three exceptional thirty-inch rams in a herd of perhaps eighty animals. They were elusive as were the black buck antelope and to a lesser degree the mouflon

Frank Schmitz

rams. Other types of game I'm sure I could have hand fed if I was carrying a grain bucket. I did harvest the three afore mentioned species. It took three days of hard searching to get the Aoudad ram. It was challenging, fun and entertaining - but we knew they could not escape and eventually we would get them. Sorry, no matter how you cut it, that is not really hunting. Had the fence not been there we most likely never would have seen those rams - ever!

Another time I went with a group of crazy road warriors on a weekend wild boar hunt in Tennessee. That place was a joke as they ran hundreds of us clowns through it a year, killing pigs. They grew pigs on a nearby farm as fast as they could raise them and turned new ones loose every week. It was not for me - but we have options as simple-minded human beings. I decided to hunt Barbary ram (instead of pig) with a bow and arrow to make it more of a challenge. The ram I shot may have let me walk up to it, but I will never know. He was bedded down when I spotted him. To make it more difficult, I was determined to try to sneak up to him from the down wind side and shoot him out of his bed if he did not detect me. That is what I did. Later, I shot a turkey with my bow, which was also very entertaining and challenging.

I have a good friend who is a big man, big enough to tip a horse I might add. He went on one of these so-called hunts, but to make it challenging his weapon of choice was a sword. Markie Demler got his boar in hand-to-hand combat. Not a method for the weak hearted or sane of mind!

In South Africa I was taken into a big enclosure once to hunt kudu. I shot at nothing in there. You've read earlier the stories about killing two free-ranging, exceptional bulls.

The fence does have its purposes; it can be fun and is. Even if you just go in to study, interact and observe game. But, any animal that is not endangered and can live wild and free in its native land should be doing just that. I pity the nutless incapable dweeb that shoots deer and elk behind a fence to get a "trophy." You cannot buy a trophy, it just won't measure up. You can lie to everyone else, but you can't lie to yourself. So every time you gaze upon your make believe trophy you will know you are a piece of shit.

I think I have beat this drum just about as long as I can, but I just noticed there is till a sound coming from it.

So I better wail the piss out of it one more time.

The INNER FORCE

I have a very good friend who raises elk. They do so because they adore them and sell the meat. It goes against my grain a little, but it's a world apart from shooting them as if they were trophies.

We all have skeletons hanging in our closets and I have my own share. We all have to feel guilt in order to understand the difference between right and wrong. Most of us pull a little crap now and again. I have shot and tagged deer with other people's tags (group hunting is legal where I did this, but sometimes the group was me, myself and I). Occasionally I put out an extra tip-up or two while ice fishing. But is that equal to going behind the fence, shooting a tame elk, taking it out and registering it as a free-ranging wild animal in the record books? And then selling stories or being a famous outdoor writer and making a living off these acts. This is where manipulation because of greed really gets wretched.

Shooting a trophy deer or elk is the most difficult and challenging accomplishment in North America hunting. Sheep are tough - but the toughest part is getting a tag where the sheep are. Harvesting a big buck or bull usually takes years. It is often a once in a lifetime feat. Inside the fence it is accomplished on any given day. What really sucks is many of the major outdoor writers make a living killing these penned animals. Think of the most famous outdoor writer on hand guns. Did he ever kill a free ranging animal? One of the most famous archers recently killed a world record elk in a western state where nobody else can kill one. Smell a rat? You bet! How tempting it is for famous writers seeking more fame and endorsements and outfitters trying to book clients to buy and release tame animals for harvest. This dilutes the records and discredits the record books and every trophy animal ever killed in fair chase.

Everybody should boycott any magazine or organization that endorses canned hunts. Write the editors and tell them to clean up their outhouse!

OK, enough! I think the drum lays lifeless before me now. I have beaten it into submission. Wait a minute I just heard a tiny beat.

Furthermore, half of what a trophy is, is having hunted the native land it resides in and interacting with the people. My memories of musk ox revolve around the fond memories of the open tundra and the Eskimo guides and children. My first elk

Frank Schmitz

reminds me of the aspen and pine-covered mountains of Colorado. For my first moose I was in the wilds of northern British Columbia with taltan Indian guides. Now if I shot an elk in Florida, what kind of memories would I have out of that hunt!

It should be illegal for these places to advertise real hunting. It misleads the public and pours gas on the anti-hunting fire. They can call it "shooting," "collecting," "harvesting" or "killing" because that is what it is. At one time I had the number four-whitetail deer in SCI. I'll bet there are at least thirty deer ahead of it from just one game farm in Michigan right now. I once was extremely proud of S.C.I., but currently am rather embarrassed by the direction it has taken. Since recording that deer I shot a Musk Ox that beat the world record by over an inch, but I have not entered it in the book. It is No. 1 in SCI and in the top thirty in B&C if entered. I have come to realize that you cannot measure a trophy with a tape. A trophy is a reflection of what you did, what you accomplished, where you went, what you saw. It is measured by what you had to do to get it. At the vary least it is a reflection of the hunt. Some times it a memory of years of hunting, or the most difficult shot, or stalk, or pack out, or of the best time you ever had. It could be a trophy even though you stepped out of your cabin or tent flap and just shot it. Because you have hunted hard for years and then it came easy. Or maybe you labored long and hard and sacrificed to get the time and money to go hunting. Then it is a trophy of your labor. A reward or a memory of your first hunt with your son or daughter, or your last hunt with your grandpa or father. A trophy can only be measured by the man who has it. It could even be a dear grandpa's shot instead of yours. A tape measure cannot score a trophy. It is that simple, just as you cannot buy a trophy. Now the last peep has been beaten out of that drum!

Heading in a completely different direction - when finances are restricted, opportunity is always welcome, especially in the hunting world. My brother, Jeff, had been working in Denver for several years where he had married and set down roots for a while before moving back to Wisconsin. His in-laws, family and friends made an annual excursion to the high country of Colorado to hunt deer and elk. They hunted on public land with rather easy access via four-wheel drive. Their success rate reflecting these facts! They had not harvested a bull elk in thirteen seasons, but had been moderately successful at taking medium to small sized mule deer bucks.

It was a get-together camp out and social event with a chance to play in the mountains. Sounded good to my youngest brother, Tim, and me. So we arranged for a surprise rendezvous with Jeff. His father-in-law would take care of all of our needs; food, camp, sleeping bags, etc. All we had to do was bring our rifles

Frank Schmitz

and personal gear. Jeff's wife, Tammy, was in on the surprise and would leave their house door open for our unexpected midnight visit. After our arrival in Denver, Tim and I made our way to Jeff's house, quietly entering not only his house and bedroom, but also his bed! We let our presence be known by doing a (politically correct term) honky pile on him. This reassured us that Jeff was not suffering from any heart problems and was ready for the mountains.

The next day we headed west stopping in Beaver Creek for fuel and at the appropriately named "Beaver Liquor" store for liquor. From there we made our way towards our destination high in the mountains. The paved road gave way to dirt and then a steep rocky trail that eventually led to the camp that Jeff's father-in-law, Jerry, had set up.

To our surprise an abnormally early snowstorm covered the mountaintop with a foot of fresh snow. The snow brought mixed blessings. Everybody knows fresh snow is a hunter's prayer being answered. But in this case we had expected mild weather, leaving us a little unprepared to say the least. We had brought along plenty of clothes, but the camp lacked proper cold weather provisions - as well as the fact that the "Boy Scouts" that set up camp....well let's just say they made some decisions that could be questioned, especially as they related to our comfort. Obviously they had pre-determined this camp site, not anticipating this early snow fall. Previous hunts had been warm to hot, so cold weather provisions were painfully lacking.

Our tent had been set up directly on top of a foot of snow that was compressed by walking on it. A thin nylon floor separated us from lying directly on the snow. Our sleeping bags featuring Mighty Mouse and Superman only came up to our mid-chest region and lacked any insulating qualities beyond their use on the living room floor. Needless to say, the first night was long, painfully cold and did not entail a bodily function called sleep. We were as snug as a bug in an ice tray. I rolled up in the fetal position in hopes of getting inside my sleeping napkin (bag) to conserve as much body heat as possible. I also wore mittens, winter hat and every piece of clothing that I had. In spite of that, I could only lay in one position for about twenty minutes before the cold from the ground would penetrate into my hip and elbow, sending bone-shattering chills through my body. Meanwhile, Jeff in his artic bag comfortably snored away while Tim and I endured our torturous conditions.

About 3:00 AM my zipper blew apart while I was shifting in the Mighty Mouse bag, ripping open the entire bottom. Instantly, I was hit with an artic blast of cold air that rapidly forced any body heat I had salvaged out of the sleeping bag. GREAT! Normally the fact that I was laying on a rock would be reason enough to complain, but it just occurred to me that this very well may be the North Pole poking me in my ass. Tim and I counted the seconds, minutes and hours tick by, only interrupted by our chattering teeth.

Finally a hint of light started to appear on the eastern horizon. I told Tim that we should take off half of these clothes and go hunting. Tim asked where I was going and I told him into the hellhole. The one place we were forewarned not to go. But as sure as a piece of schpec, (animal fat) is better served on a tent wall than in a bowl of chili, this was the place for us.

The hellhole was a seemingly bottomless pit located directly behind camp. We had been forewarned that whatever we do, do not go into the hellhole. If you go in there, you will never get back out. I figured if it's a date with the devil, bring it on because I sure could use the heat. The plan we devised was to hunt three quarters of the way down on each side. I would drop through the bottom to the opposite side. As we descended in the hellhole, we quickly realized it was much deeper than it appeared. But down we went. After an hour, I departed from Tim as we wished each other good luck.

Another hour had passed before I could see the bottom of this brutal pit. I came across a game trail perhaps two hundred feet above the creek that trickled through the valley. I had side hilled along quietly on it for twenty minutes when I heard a crashing sound high above me. My first impression was that a dead, rotting tree had collapsed under its own weight, smashing to the forest floor. But the crashing continued. Next I thought it could be a herd of mule deer charging down the mountain. I ran ahead trying to intercept the animals causing such a racket. After having covered several hundred feet, I was more in line with the rapidly descending herd, so I thought! I looked up the mountain and saw a large rack bobbing in and out of sight as it charged down the hill. It was a bull elk, obviously spooked off the top and coming down like a runaway freight train. I ducked under a large spruce tree to hide and position myself for a shot.

Frank Schmitz

    Within an instant, the mighty beast was upon me - covering over sixteen feet of ground in each powerful leap, while going right through anything in its way. From where I was standing, the elk was positioned at ten o'clock when his feet hit the ground and my scope locked in on his front shoulder. Without hesitation, my gun fired but the elk showed no response as he leaped forward again. He was straight in front of me at the twelve o'clock position when his feet hit the ground the next time. Again my rifle fired at his boiler room with no ill effects.

    Instantly the massive creature leapt airborne again, landing sixteen feet down the hill, now at the two o'clock position. My gun responded simultaneously as the elk rocketed forward. Seldom do I have four rounds in my gun, but that day I had loaded the chamber and the magazine. My fourth and final round was delivered as the elk completed his next, but last leap. The bull crumbled to the ground, dead. All four rounds had either double lunged him or pierced his fuel pump! He just kept going not knowing he was already dead.

    The forest returned to its tranquil state as I admired the biggest, grandest beast I had killed to date. I knelt beside him, admiring his mass and beauty while my hands softly glided over his impressive antlers. This great beast humbled me, as did my subsiding adrenaline rush. I knelt there shaking like a sinner standing at the pearly gates while I inhaled a full gamut of emotions; exhilaration, happiness, sadness, triumph, and defeat. Good fortune is always a mixed blessing, not only of emotions, but also of the reality that lies in front of me. Now the work begins; quartering, caping, dehorning, butchering, deboning. Then with the animal on our backs, we must ascend out of the appropriately named hellhole.

The pain and exhaustion that followed for the next twenty-four hours would make sleeping on the snow easy. It also solidified the meaning of a trophy. Although bigger and grander bulls came my way in the future, none will ever surpass the immeasurable trophy value of my first bull.

Tonight as I sipped a couple African Castle Beers, Nixon strolled up to tell me - a leopard had been at the bait but did not eat. I think he will come back and strike tonight. If it does we will be off to a new place, Gonarezhou Park concession. The guy baiting there since the hunt started is another African man who has two wives. He has eight children. I cannot remember or pronounce his name, so have started calling him Double Dick in honor of his double duties. Hopefully, we may be seeing Double Dick soon!

Frank Schmitz

June 8

I have been writing since 3:00 AM. It is near dawn and my seventy-sheet notebook is full. Nixon said we would have to go to town to get lined paper. That means I will be without paper for several days. I'll have to go on memory and scribble on anything I can find. I could just go on my memory, but my mind is like good whiskey - It does not last long, in one ear and out the other, if you know what I mean! I was going to tell you about that….umm….you know that…..oh whatever, the hell with it! If that ever happens to you, we are in the same boat I'm afraid, and it looks like it's leaking and we are far from shore.

I found out last night that the water in Chipimbi and Nyala camps is no good to drink. I have been brushing my teeth and taking sinus medication for eight days with this water!

Nixon just shook his head. "No good Frank. Water no good. Why you think we have bottled water." True bottled water is available in the eating area. All the bottles' seals are broken so they obviously are being filled on site somewhere. Nobody ever mentioned that the running water in my quarters was not good to drink. My daughter Angie always says "Assume - Never Assume!" I guess she is right about that one. But I'm used to drinking water from just about any stream in the mountains I hunt back at home in North Central Idaho. As a matter of fact I always have a cup in my pack, rather than a bottle of water when guiding.

Oh well, my butt is holding together so maybe my system is an unfit environment for the African bugs that infest it!

We returned to the Chipimbi Camp after a morning of buffalo chasing. We received word that one of the baits had been hit in a concession that borders the park.

Nixon, Dixon, Steven and I loaded up the Land Rover and took off. It is a two and one-half hour drive to the area, but with Nixon behind the wheel we probably will make it in two. He drives like the late Dale Earnhart, so I assume that we are setting a new track record wherever we travel. The roads are gravel and bumpy at this time of year as we bounce and clang our way to our destination. My passenger window (which is on the left side) vibrates open. I periodically pull it back up by hand. It is a reflection of the life in Africa.

Frank Schmitz

Soon we are at our destination. The entrance is cleverly disguised to ward off intruders. The entrance is marked by an elephant's skull mounted on top of three wooden posts opposite of where you turn in. The property is fenced off with steel fence posts and steel cable. It is a three-strand fence, but in the area where we access the property, the steel cable is not attached to the posts. The weight of a man standing on the wire pushes it down enough to allow our vehicle to enter. The dirt trail we drive on is the boundary between the national park and our hunting area.

I would expect game to be particularly abundant here but see no animals as we enter or leave. The abundance and variety of game seems to have been the greatest at the Nyala Camp. Surprisingly, that camp is the least protected and the furthest distance from the park. At this park, the second largest in Zimbabwe, I expected a grand and unusual landscape; big rivers, waterfalls and mountainous topography. Instead it was a flat, brushy savanna - even less rugged than the Chipimbi Camp country. Nothing about it indicated that it was a park except a sign on the main road.

Shortly after entering the hunting concession we located one of the bait sites and blinds they had built. We were off once again after a short stop. I noticed big piles of "dirt" on the road as we traveled down the road separating the park from the hunting concession. The piles were up to eighteen inches high and equally as wide. They were scattered about like a series of land mines. Upon approaching them I realized they were giant piles of dung. Elephant dung! There were massive, almost circular imprints two feet across or larger on the dusty road. These were the most impressive tracks I had seen since the time I stood with both my size twelve boots inside a Kodiak bear's hind foot impression. I must admit that giant bear track was more intimidating. Non-the-less, my eyes searched the bush for a glimpse at one of these jumbos. I hope to see one in the wild soon.

We arrived at the bait site a short time later. The bait appeared to be part of the giraffe I had shot and was suspended fifty yards from the blind about seven feet up in a tree. The plan was to allow a leopard to come back to this previously discovered kill. When it climbs the tree to feast, I would let him have it.

The blind is a piece of art in itself. A square frame built of limbs. Other limbs are woven in and out of the frame until it creates a solid wall of branches and leaves. You cannot see in or out of it except for two small peepholes designed to look, shoot or shine a light through.

In Zimbabwe it is legal to hunt day and night. Leopards are nocturnal animals so you can expect them to arrive after dark. The way its supposed to work is when we hear the leopard climb the tree and start eating, Nixon turns on the spot light and I shoot the cat. Sounds quite easy, but here is the problem. The cat first prowls the area checking for scent. If he thinks all is well he may come to the bait sometime that night. If he does, any strange noise will send him on his way. When the light hits him, he will jump and run within a few seconds. This means first the P.H. has to get him in the light rapidly. Second, the hunter has to find him in his scope - fast. Third, the cat has to be in a position to offer a clean killing shot.

All of these things do not come together quickly and smoothly very often. It seems you would have an advantage if you're a seasoned and skilled poacher. On a trial run, I fumbled around for a long time trying to find the bait in my scope. Leopards are extremely dangerous if your shot is bad. That is when your life hangs in the balance. That is what you want to avoid!

It was 4:00 PM when Nixon and I settled into our blind. Nixon brought chairs to sit in, padded seats, and a bottle of water to stifle a cough. Coke-a-cola was on hand for a refreshment. The spotting light was set-up on a rest. We checked over the view to the bait. My .416 balanced on a towel through the opening, positioned to the tree where we hoped the spotted cat would be. We went over everything in detail like preparing for an attack on a foreign country. Nixon's final instructions....Now don't shoot unless everything is perfect. A leopard is a very dangerous animal. We don't want to wound him.

"Entering Leopord Blind"

We get as comfortable as possible and try to sit motionless for the upcoming six hours. I hate sitting. I can't stand sitting! My ass gets sore. It was designed for standing up or lying down.

My brother, Tim, is probably getting revenge on me since I dropped him off this year in the mountains of Idaho to sit in a rather uncomfortable tree stand until dark. It was 11:00 AM when I left him. We were bear hunting and his bait had been destroyed. The hunter I had left in this stand the year before needed to wait all of ten minutes for a chocolate colored brown bear to show.

The INNER FORCE

Apparently the bear was at the bait when we showed up, sneaking off as we approached. The hunter climbed into the tree stand. I followed him up to see if everything was working out for him. He was hunting with a bow and arrow.

Everything was fine so I climbed down and left, not knowing the bear sat in the bush watching all of this. The good thing was that bear could not count - two go up the tree; one comes down and leaves. So he thought the coast was clear. Minutes later he comes strolling along to see what we brought him for lunch. Unfortunately for the hunter - hisarrow goes astray; lucky for the bear - the bear escapes. I figured the same bear was back this year and Tim would score early in the day. Instead he got his ass stretched and flattened for eight hours. Pure torture, no bear ever showed. Oh well, that's hunting! Sometimes it sucks!

The theory for killing a leopard is to hang bait in a tree. Then, if we get good tracks, build a grass or stick blind and sit motionless in it. Finally, if the leopard shows up in the dark, does not detect you and goes to the bait without walking into your blind, you shoot him out of the tree. In America, we go in the tree and shoot the predator as it approaches, using the tree for safety. Here after you shoot the leopard and he hits the ground, you hope he does not run into the blind. Better yet, you hope he's dead when he hits the ground. Tracking a wounded leopard in darkness is extremely dangerous - especially when the fricken Brits have your gun!

Well, now my ass was flattening. I was motionless for a long time, but soon grew uncomfortable. Darkness was approaching as several hours passed. Nixon and I sat....and sat. Did I mention before that I hate sitting! I hate tree stands. I hate waiting. I would look like a tap dancer if you ever videotaped me in a tree stand deer hunting and played it in fast forward. When I sit, my nose itches and runs. I have to scratch, move my leg, wiggle my arm and pick my butt. I have to do this! All without making noise! It sucks.

More time creaks by - slowly. Time stops when you have to sit. Instead of it turning darker and getting later, it goes back towards morning. If I did this for ten years straight, I would be back in high school. Well, maybe it would take more like thirty years, but who is counting. The time really does go forward, but like a snail, a starving snail, a starving snail with broken legs, a starving snail with broken legs trying to carry his whole damn family...of 564 kids on his back none-the-less. Okay, got the point!

Frank Schmitz

    I sit watching two flies humping on my arm. Dang, these damn flies are having a better time than me! Don't be laying any fricken eggs in my arm you little shitters. Holy crap they are having such a good time I can hear them panting.

    I look up at Nixon; he's got big, huge white eyes with that "we are in deep shit" face! The leopard is standing an arms length away from me, only separated by the woven branches. I can hear him breathe. I can smell his stinky garbage eating breath - the breath of raw flesh. We dare not breathe. I try to stop my heart from pounding. I can hear my damned watch – tick, tick, tick, tick. It sounds like, eat me, eat me, eat me. I am concentrating so hard on not breathing and stopping my watch and heart that suddenly I no longer hear him panting. The smell of death drifts off. The leopard has disappeared....silently, motionlessly gone.

    It seemed like seconds took minutes, minutes took hours, and hours took days. I sat there for a few weeks I guess. The night was black. I could see just as well with my eyes closed as open.

The INNER FORCE

There was no moon and would be no moon for a while. (The moon was in the northern hemisphere and we were not!) When dark came it was as black as a coal mine shaft two hundred feet below the surface. I could not make out the silhouette of my arm or gun much less my P.H. sitting right next to me.

Then at about 9:00 PM, three hours past dark, I heard the leopard again. He was at the bait making a gurgling, throaty growl. The noise sounded somewhat like a pig. He inspected the tree and moved around for ten minutes. Again, we dare not breathe. Then all was quiet. What was he doing? Sitting by the tree contemplating his fate?

Things must not have seemed kosher and he was tip-toeing around the area - inspecting it of course. We had no clue what he was up to. Then a snarling growl comes from the blackness. I almost jumped out of my shoes while trying not to make a sound. The leopard is right in front of me - six feet away - just on the other side of the blind that separates us. We do not twitch a muscle as we wonder what the cat is doing now. We sat motionless until ten o'clock. The leopard is gone.

He figured out our little scam. Asta la vista was the final snarl he made in our faces. I cannot help but feel he is still watching us as we make our way back to the truck,. I feel his gold-green eyes cutting through my back. I feel his hate and wish I had my A-bolt.

We pad along silently in the dark, thinking and wondering about the leopard that lurks somewhere around us in the darkness. The darkness reminds me of early morning elk hunts in Idaho as my mind drifts back to an encounter back home last season.

The morning was cold as we saddled our horses and gathered our gear together. I knew the heavy timber would be cloaked in blackness since only a few stars shone in the night sky. The moon had descended hours ago against a black horizon. Using my headlamp I looked for gloves because it was only forty degrees with a heavy dew at our elevation. Surely there will be morning frost where we are about to go. It's 3:30 AM. We have time for another cup of hot coffee.

At 3:45 my left foot slips into my stirrup as I swing my body onto my saddle. My hunter follows suit on his horse, Cinnamon, with his bow slung over his shoulder. Our head lamps are turned off. For the next two hours I will trust my life to the sure feet of my faithful partner, Thud. Thud has traveled these trails in this

Frank Schmitz

backcountry for twenty some years. He is more intimate with this land than a man will ever be. The next couple of hours he will be my night vision, my eyes, my pilot. I will be the co-pilot, only occasionally offering directional advice. Thoughts of bull elk dance in our heads as we ride across the meadow in the scant starlight.

"Me, with my first best horse - Thud"

The INNER FORCE

A black silhouette in the night sky guides me as the North Star once guided the three wise men. The black shadow I ride towards is an old yellow pine called the "bee tree." From there, Thud instinctively turns left, plodding up the phone line trail towards dark timber.

The glow of lantern light at our camp (the historic Gilmore Ranch) fades away behind us, just as it had for countless hunters over the past decades. The ghosts of past outfitters ride upon my shoulders; Hal Miller, Buck Barton and most recently Chuck Neil. The stories of fabulous hunts gone by play through my mind - some theirs, some mine and the hunters that made them happen. I wonder if today will be a new chapter in the colorful history of the Gilmore Ranch or just another day of adventure. I wonder what the legends of recent years and my top clients, Gene Primasing and Willie Walsh, are doing and wish they were with me. I know they also wish they could ride along today.

Frank Schmitz

    We ride under the thick canopy of mature timber. It blocks out what little starlight we had. We ride ahead quietly, in total darkness, unable to see even the shadow of our horse's head. I close my eyes, allowing myself to feel the trail, only having to know when to direct Thud from turning onto trails of lesser destinations. He too, knows we are going to ride high, but still tries to trick me into a shorter ride to a less grueling tie-up point.

    After an hour we begin to ascend the steep trail to the high country. I tuck my head down into the collar of my wool coat as the falling temperatures bite at my nose and cheeks. Thirty minutes latter the darkness slowly relinquishes its black grip on this mountainous landscape. The shadows of pre-dawn are upon us. The cold morning air cracks at our fingers and toes... one thing I really do not enjoy! Freezing extremities is the thought of the moment. The forest is silent except for the sound of shoed hoofs clanking against the rocky trail.

    As we near the crest, I cow call occasionally, hoping to trick or possibly delay elk into lingering around. Their curiosity may allow us to see them. The witching hour is upon us - that time of half-light and half-dark - when I hear the first bull squeal in the canyon below us. We are nearing our preplanned destination, Wing Creek, when I see movement ahead of us. It's the buff tan tail ends of cows trotting across our trail and away. Four of them pass before a larger animal crosses. I can see his big, heavy main beams graced with long ivory tipped tines. Its show time!

    We quickly dismount our trusty old steeds, tying them to a tree. The underbrush seems to be illuminated from the white layer of frost painted on its surface. My hunter, Chuck, gathers up his compound bow and quiver of arrows as I sort out my work tools; bugle cow call, binoculars, plus a few toys like a rangefinder and cover scent. We hustle up the trail as fast and quiet as possible, studying wind conditions as we go.

    The elk have moved up in a draw above us. The mountain maple underbrush is dense under the heavy canopy of fir. Wind conditions are advantages as we sneak into the little drainage, looking for a place to set up. A small bench opens up on our right with good cover around it.

    Chuck eases up about thirty yards ahead of me as I rake a sapling with a piece of dead wood. My bugle than sings an elk song - a short, high-pitched squeal that I hope translates into "I'm a young punk and I want your girls!" The response is instantaneous as the big bull bugles back with a throaty, raspy and much deeper squeal. He commands "Clear out punk, if you know what's good for you!" The serenade has begun. I respond with another short bugle, but throw in a few quick cow calls, too. The big boy bellows back another warning. Hopefully, he thinks this punk has some cows.

There is branch breaking, some more raking of limbs and cow calling before I submit to silence. The enraged bull now bellows out in a long deep bugle followed by four throaty chuckles. Oh boy, his temperature is rising. I mimic with a short "Meee-you." Its bull talk I've heard before - a bull saying, "Come on girls lets get out of here." To this I add cow and calf calls with the snapping of breaking branches. We wonder if the angered wapiti will take the bait.

Shortly we are delighted to hear a loud, raspy bugle from above the six deep chuckles followed by crashing brush. The big boy is coming like a love crazed sheik determined to expand his harem. I duck down behind a tree and some brush, responding with a cow call. There is crashing brush and breaking branches as his mighty crown comes into view on the bench above us. His thick burly beams are stained walnut brown with long tines polished at the tips to a glistening ivory white. He is a majestic brute with a thick dark mud caked cape and a tan face filled with the violence that lurks within.

The impressive beast lowers his head to a small Christmas tree type fir, venting his rage upon it. His tines snap branches as he rakes his antlers up and down, stripping its bark as he goes. We watch in awe as he demolishes this now dead tree. The message he is sending says, "Hey girls I am the man for you, forget about that wimp you're with."

Chuck stands motionless to my right, draped in his camouflaged skin of threads. His face is painted olive and forest green. He patiently awaits an opportunity of a lifetime. His heart pounds with anticipation as he wonders if he can maintain his composure. The bull must step forward a couple yards to present a shot. A down draft fills the air with the unmistakable stench of rutting bull elk. He has an intimidating muscle bound neck and shoulders. His majestic face is graced with world class massive branch's of bone atop - his crown that translates into "I am the King."

I let out a soft purr on my cow call, hoping that it says "Hey tall dark and handsome, I'm over here. Come to me, baby." The

Frank Schmitz

bull takes a step in my direction through the brush that shields him. I hunker down to hide as I watch him stretch his thick heavy neck towards me. His ears are cupped forward and his eyes are staring to my location. He wants to see this sexy thing!

I hear a soft thump behind me - almost like a big ball of yarn dropping onto a firm mattress. My mind races, thinking I hope an elk isn't sneaking in behind me. I turn my head slowly scanning

The INNER FORCE

the thick and shadowy underbrush as the first rays of morning sun filter through the trees. The soft beams of sunlight dance against the wet frosty leaves, illuminating a silky piece of artwork a spider has woven. The bull makes a soft grunt "Erwooo - Where are you honey?" I redirect my attention to the bull with my cow call clenched between my teeth, I exhale softly through it, "Meee You." To his ears the sound has to be like that of a beautiful women sitting on a barstool, letting the split of her skirt fall open, gently shifting her legs apart and exposing her warm inner thighs. Right over here baby!

The bull cautiously lifts his front leg and steps forward, straining to see into my location. With his undivided attention focused on me, he does not notice the trembling hands of the bow hunter to his side as he draws his string back, breaking his bow over into a shooting position. His bow now at full draw, he only needs the bull to take another half step and then "he is his."

Again, the soft padded sound comes from behind me. I get this feeling that something is watching me. I slowly turn my head a second time, peering into the frosty brush. Some of the leaves glisten with drops of water forming at their tips as the frost thaws. Now the spider web reflects with teardrops forming on its silk strands. Left of center in the web is a transparent wet spot that looks slightly out of place. My eyes strain to focus on it. It is not part of the web, but beyond it. My eyes struggle to refocus through the web into the shadows, at this translucent amber spot.

As me eyes readjust, two spots appear, then a third. They are wet, glassy and circular spots...golden in color as if to be ripe wheat, ready for harvest. Suddenly as if a thousand spiders were crawling out of my pants and up my back a tremor of surprise ascends my vertebra. As my eyes focus on the spots ten yards behind me, nature's camouflage finally gives way and betrays the beast. As if staring into a pool of water at a reflection, there is an image that stares back. It is not my image. It is the image of another beast. Behind me, crouched and ready to pounce is a pair of animals. These eyes, too are trying to focus back into my pale blue eyes through the sparkling web. We are locked in a momentary stare-down, tying to identify each other.

These eyes analyze their prey, trying to figure out how to expedite the attack. Trying to determine my body position so as to be able to pounce on my back and lock powerful jaws across my

Frank Schmitz

throat. Figuring out how to squeeze the air from my body while his mate clamps down on my face to render me helpless.

The hair on the back of my neck stands up as the wave of surprise sweeps across the back of my head. With my eyes locked into the horrifying toothy faces of this pair of predators - a gasp of surprise exhales from inside of me. A sound that transfers through my cow call. No longer does it sound like "I'm right here baby, come and get me." It sounds more like that of a thug sticking up a Seven Eleven store.

The forest explodes into whirl of sound and motion. There is the sound of a reeling bull with antlers knocking against branches. There is the twang of a bow as an arrow leaves it. There is an explosion of muscle as a pair of predators leap into motion. There is crashing going up and away as the wapiti exits to parts unknown. There is the clatter of an aluminum shaft, harmlessly sailing through branches. There is a blur of departing large grey silhouettes and thick bushy tails loping down the mountain as the Canadian timber wolves decide to hunt something that doesn't stink as bad as a human.

There is a trembling and disappointed bow hunter standing in confusion. Wondering about my last call selection. There is a guide lying in the bush below him with his heart racing from an unexpected adrenaline rush. That is the surprise of unexpected guests at the dinner table! We all got to live another day in Mother Nature's cycle of life and death. For life to continue tomorrow there must be a winner and a looser. That's the law of nature. Such are the emotions of a hunter, and of the hunted.

I refocus on the blackness that surrounds me in Africa as I listen to our footsteps pounding against the dirt trail. Standing face to face, staring into the penetrating eyes of a predator etches vivid pictures in your mind. Their eyes stare into your eyes - reading your mind, seeking to sense your fear. It is haunting and telepathic thing. Show fear and bring them upon you. Show courage and they will bow down, just like aggressive but domestic dogs. They read your mind, sense if you have control and act upon that sense.

Walking in the dark on this road, I wonder if the cat lays in the shadows, studying us as we stride away. I can feel his eyes staring at me. I wonder if he can stare through the back of my head in order to pick my brain and read my mind. This is what intrigues me about the wild cats of the world. They call to me. They beckon me to hunt them as if in a game of chess. Tonight the cats mighty

The INNER FORCE

paw slides his bishop forward, looks into my eyes as only a cat can, and softly purrs out "Check!"

    But now it is my turn. The game is not over!
    We drive back toward Chipimbi Camp, arriving at 1:00 AM. The plan is to rise again at 5:00 AM. The girls want to know if I would like supper. "No thanks." I respond. White Bwana wants to sleep now.

Frank Schmitz

June 9

Morning comes quickly. It is the coldest morning so far. Last night, I hid under my blanket because my head was freezing. But then I could not breathe and would need fresh air. Eventually I wrapped my head in a blanket with my face exposed to the cold night air, keeping my head warm while breathing fresh African oxygen.

All too soon it was daybreak. I take my morning ritual walk to the fire circle, sip a cup of coffee and listen to the jungle wake up. One of the natives is responsible for always having a fire burning before dawn for the clientele to gather around. It is definitely the best time of the day. I wonder why our busy life forces us to regularly sleep through it. The best things in life are right in front of us every day, but we often waste them away. The people here may be monetarily poor, but are rich at heart! In this predawn, they are huddled around the cookhouse fire and I hear them chatting, laughing, occasionally singing or chanting and enjoying life.

I sit at the fire ring, warming my hands on my porcelain coffee mug while sipping the eye-opener down. I listen to the jungle slowly awaken and watch pre-dawn illuminate the eastern sky. This time of day is magic. My only regret is that I sit alone, having nobody to share it with. No companionship, no camaraderie with buddies, no fellowship, nobody with which to share the daily events - the highs and lows.

I think it sure sucks to be the rest of the world because they are missing out! It is good to watch Africa awaken; too bad you can't be with me.

Nixon arrives for breakfast; we eat another fabulous meal, finish our coffee and discuss the day's plans. "Let's go chase buffalo" thoughts are racing through my mind. Luckily for us, the buffalo did not travel very far staying in the vicinity of the scarce water.

We drive around looking for spoor and we find it. Fresh spoor. Dung that is warm and the smell of buffalo urine is strong. Nixon, Dixon and I take up the tracks with the Grim Reaper. We follow the spoor for two hours. At one point I hear a distant rumble of hoofs, the sound of a big herd of animals. We are sure to be among

Frank Schmitz

the buffalos shortly. We carry on another mile and then another. Several more hours go by. The sun is getting high and very hot.

We carry on as sweat runs down my face and back. No buffalo. Where did they go? Suddenly I see unwanted signs of civilization - a power line overhead and a road with a ten-wire fence. The fence is a buffalo proof. We have traveled to the edge of their domain. Earlier I stated how the government set aside fifteen percent of the land in preserves (parks) for the animals; and another fifteen percent for animals were grazing and human activities such as hunting are allowed. These areas are around the perimeters of the preserves. The rest of the country is for humans, farming, livestock, etc.

Buffalo carry foot and mouth disease which is deadly to cattle. We are at the buffalos' borderline. The government will not allow creatures like buffalo, elephants, rhinos and the like past here. Otherwise they would destroy crops and the native's meager livelihoods. This policy is far, far more liberal than our game management in the U.S.A. We exterminated our buffalo and grizzly bear from the entire western U.S. Today we only allow them to roam free in Yellowstone Park. Do not leave or we will kill you, is the rule. This is perhaps one hundred thousandths of their original range. We have no other room for them in our country (except for domesticated buffalo herds on farms). We have an idiotic concept about preserving our game, our Disneyland management policies.

Cougar, for example, are protected in California as if they are a threatened animal. Do not hunt them or they will be gone. Protect them, domesticate them and when they lose fear of man, they intrude on developed land. They come prowling, killing our pet dogs, cats, and occasionally a human. Cougars no longer fear these things because their wild instinct is gone. Then we say that this cougar is "acting up. This is a problem animal. He must be culled out and destroyed." So we send the authorities after them with hounds and they kill the 'bad' cat; the one that was not conforming to our Disneyland expectations. They kill more cougar this way now in California than were ever killed during the years of legal hunting seasons. It does not make much sense. These animals cannot be protected from themselves and their instincts. Man is always outsmarting himself. We are a simple minded lot!

Anyway - back to the buffalo hunting. We had followed the herd to this restricted perimeter. They had traveled north and turned back into their domain, away from the barricade that protects the rest of the world from them. We followed for six hours, but the buffalo were gone. They had vanished and we gave up the chase.

We spot a croc as we near camp and the lake that borders it. He is sunbathing on a sand bar 250 yards from shore. We study him for along time. Nixon continually probes me to shot. I keep saying he is too far. The target of his spine is too small. "You can do it. You can make the shot," he eggs me on. I take a rest, study it some more, and after a half hour Nixon has convinced me that I can hit a one inch target at 250 yards. I squeeze the trigger and the bullet barks into the sand just under the twelve foot beast. In one mighty flip, he disappears in the water along with the other three sunbathers that had been out.

Nixon laughs aloud, "You scared the hell out of them, didn't you."

Yes, real funny! Actually Dixon and I think we heard the shot hit. The croc spun his head towards us before disappearing the opposite direction in the water, but you can't hardly hunt these dinosaurs at this range, much less kill them. A 300 grain bullet zipping a flesh wound into the croc is nothing more than a puncture wound...daily occurrences for them as the toothy creatures battle each other in their game of "king of the hill," or more appropriate "king of the mud flat."

It amazes me how many people assist in an African safari. I have my P. H. Nixon and usually three trackers with us at all times. There is no need for all of them, but I think they just have nothing else to do and figure we can always use extra eyes. At camp, there is a waiter, a cook, and a cleaning lady. Three or four others look after camp, raking and watering the grass and plants. There are another four or five men that are skinners and fleshers that clean hides and horns. Luckily these guys are used to working for almost nothing. Most of the natives live in extreme poverty, owning only the clothing on their backs. Some have no shoes; just strong, calloused bare feet. But it is all they know so they are quite happy.

There are obvious classes of people here, with the whites forming the upper class. There are middle and lower class whites, but none that fall as far as the low class black population. Some blacks have broken the class barriers and are middle to upper class. Nixon lives rather impressively and is highly regarded by

Frank Schmitz

the other blacks. He is building a huge new house that is costing four million dollars Zimbabwean, which equals to $70,000 U.S. The house is comparable in size to my lodge which has eight bedrooms. The home he lives in now looks very nice from the outside and has a beautifully landscaped yard. It is surrounded by a wrought iron high fence and gated driveway with three watchdogs standing guard (which surprises me). Nixon has six children, three boys and three girls. The boys are all in the hunting business. His second daughter, a beautiful brilliant young girl, is going to the University of Wisconsin Green Bay next year. It is the same school my second daughter, Sara, attended. That really floored me; not only that of all places she would go there - but that she would have this opportunity in the first place.

With me on this trip I had two hats; one of the almighty Green Bay Packers and a second, a gift from my daughter that had UWGB on it. I gave the packer hat to Nixon and the second hat to his daughter....appropriate, since this was the university she was about to attend. I warned her of cold and snow, elements she has not yet seen. And I warned her of freedom for women, another element she has not yet seen.

I never had the opportunity to attend college. School to me was like being in prison. A communist society where everyone was instructed to do the same thing. Read the same crap. Buzzer sounds and herd to the next room! Repetition with limited opportunity for freedom of expression. I remember being in Room 108 doing a final exam as spring approached outside the "compound." Suddenly the fist robin of the year landed on a windowsill and began to chirp away - calling to us or perhaps laughing at us, but for sure showing off its freedom. I remember gazing at that bird and forgetting about the test in front of me, thinking why can't I be that bird? It would be great to be free flying and living outside.

We go back to the camp and I take a short nap. Waking, I decide to walk to the compound. It is a work area. There are several buildings where twenty locals repair trucks and do maintenance. It is also the location of Nixon's house and I want to give his beautiful smiling daughter some candy.

I must say that a white man walking on the road draws attention in this part of Africa. Several black men, some barefooted, stop to ask if everything is all right.

I reply, "Yes."

"Where are you going?"

"Nixon's house."
"Okay."

Over the next half mile, I repeat this conversation several times. Then a pickup truck driven by Nancy, the white woman who is Trevor's wife from Nyala camp, and her son drive up in an old pick-up truck.

She asks, "What is wrong."
"Nothing."
"Where are you going?"
"Nixon's house."
"Everything alright?"
"Yes."
"Are you sure?"
"Yes."
"What business must you take care of?"
"I am just bringing his daughter candy and thought I would exercise off my lunch. Okay?"
"You sure everything is alright?"
"Yes."

I proceed down the road and within fifteen minutes or so another car pulls up. The car is a newer sedan of sorts, a luxury car and the windows tinted too dark to see into it. The driver's window slides down to expose a dark haired, middle-aged women with a concerned look about her face. To my amusement it's a white woman in her forties. This is more white folks than I have seen in a week and a half. This woman is fairly attractive with hair obviously dyed to hide her impending gray. She asks if I am all right.

"Yes..." The previous interrogation continues.
Then she says, "Please get in the car and let me take you to Nixon's house."

I respond, "I can walk."
"No, I must insist you come with me!"
"Are you sure?"
"You, get in please!"

So I do. On the way to Nixon's house, I find out she is Lloyd Yatsman's ex-wife. (Lloyd is the owner of the safari company.) She is selling her house and moving to New Zealand. I do not ask if she feels safe here or not because I no longer care. I know I feel perfectly safe and have no concerns for my welfare. The local folks are all very polite. Every native person I meet greets

Frank Schmitz

me with "Good morning, Sir or good afternoon, Sir. How are you today?" I respond that I am fine and ask back. "I am fine also," is the customary response. In the past week and a half only one native woman replied that she was okay.

I asked, "You are not fine?" She looked back, obviously not having a good day and said she was okay.

I think that some white folks that felt threatened have left and some more will leave. Many just cannot drop everything and many are not financially able to pick up and go. This is their home, their lives. They have worked side by side with the locals and are absolutely not threatened in any way. They have nothing to fear and will not be confronted. Some people who took advantage of the natives for a long time and refuse to give an inch probably will end up in a confrontation. There are bad situations I am sure, but they are widespread and uncommon.

Yet Nixon, a black man himself, has a high security fence around his yard, a steel gate, steel bars on his windows and three large watch dogs behind the fence. My cabin door is locked when I leave. Often I am locked out of my room when I return from the day's activities. The trucks are loaded at night. So there maybe more going on than meets the eye. Yet the people looking after me want desperately for me to be comfortable and feel secure. I'm not sure if they lock everything so I won't worry about my stuff. They certainly do not know that I leave everything unlocked and open at home. Or, that I share my house with strangers for a living. I am a trusting fool! But it is my way. I do know one thing, a white man walking down a road is an uncommon sight, a reason for concern, something must be wrong! This definitely draw's attention.

We crossed fresh bull sable spoor early this afternoon and hope to track him to within shooting range. We've turned our comrades loose on the trail. The trackers move ahead of us at a slow pace and then jog, fingers point, heads nod. They track as a team, each finding a scant occasional sign, but together they rapidly cover lots of ground. The trackers are, Bones, Gravedigger and the Grim Reaper. The Reaper is the lead man flanked by Gravedigger and Bones as they pick up subtle turns in the animal's trail.

I figure these guys are not on this earth for long since trackers are the first line of defense in an attack. Armed with two knives, their destiny is bleak. Meanwhile they revel in the honorary positions they hold in the tribe. We cover several miles of savanna as the sun pushes upward into the morning sky.

Animal activity has seized for the time being as the game lays low until evening. African critters know when to conserve their energy if they intend to survive the day. The only movement in this desert is the trackers and us, as we seek the sables' refuge. We move forward and remain silent with a slight swirl of dust kicked up from our shuffling feet being the only evidence of our presence. A wise man once said, "When in Rome do as the Romans do." That is how hunting often is! Most times the surest bet is to go with the locals' proven techniques. Deer hunters in the West still hunt or use spot and stalk methods - while looking down their noses at stump sitters from the Mid-West - whom look down their noses at the stump sitters in tiny cabins with automatic feeders to the South - whom look down their noses at houndsmen running deer in the Southeast.

It is important to maintain our own ethics while being flexible enough to use proven methods of hunting in different regions or countries. Of course, you can stick to your own individuality and only do it your way. That is why we have rifle hunters, muzzle load hunters and archery hunters. Even this choice of weapons does not satisfy all of us in creating the challenge we crave. Enter handgun hunters, archery hunters that use recurves or long bows, and muzzleloaders that remain traditionalists.

One should be careful not to condemn a method he does not understand or endorse, as long as it is fair chase. Houndsmen versus bait sitters are a classic example. I have had houndsmen challenge the manhood of bait sitters. I have been told it tests a man to follow hounds across a mountain and that only the strong survive to stand at the base of the tree. Bait hunters are just shooting fish in a barrel. Not to your surprise, I have often hunted both ways. I have seen hunters not make it to the tree and I have expended all I have had to make it there on more than one occasion. Sometimes I think that the last 500 yards are the toughest because you can climb for what seems like days to cover it. Of course, it would be easier to climb if I wasn't tripping over my tongue all the time while my heart was jumping from my chest, beating louder than the University of Wisconsin Marching Band during the fifth quarter!

My first mountain lion hunt in Idaho tested our mettle - twice. The first day we ran a two-day old track, chasing the tom for seven

Frank Schmitz

or eight miles through knee to waist deep snow. That day we treed and I passed up two tom lions in hope for a monster. Terri hunted with me. We both were over dressed, wearing heavy wool clothes that became soaking wet during the day. The long climb out of the canyon to our snowmobiles took until 10 PM, five hours past last light. We where exhausted and would have died of hypothermia if we would not have made it to our sleds.

One week later we cut another big, two-day old track in the same hellhole. This time we shed lots of cloths before striking out. Seven hours later the tracks turned fresh. at 4:30 PM I dispatched a big lion that would stand as NO. 9 all time in SCI record book. The struggle through knee-deep and falling snow for eight hours had us drenched in sweat and melted snow. After being shot, the large tom had jumped the tree and raced perhaps one hundred yards down the mountain to the bottom of the draw. There he lay, submerged in the fresh cold creek.

The INNER FORCE

Darrel Weddle who was hunting with us reached into the creek to retrieve the mighty tom. With the speed of greased lightening the cat's front paw shot up from his watery grave and hooked its protruding claws into Darrel's forearm. We grabbed onto Darrell in a tug of war battle until the claws tore through his long sleeves, freeing him of the cats desperate strangle hold. We decided to let him breath water for a while longer before pulling him from his grave!

Frank Schmitz

After a photo session, skinning, butchering and packing, the last minutes of daylight found us miles from our snow cats. Terri, Gary Haight (our guide) and I beat feet to try to get back to the base of that mountain. Snow set in before dark. Darrel, our other companion, experienced guide and outfitter went after some of the dogs that had taken up another track. This time it was near midnight when we reached our snow sleds.

Lucky for Darrel he could build a fire, because he didn't make it out that night! By the time he retrieved his dogs it was already after dark and snowing hard. He was ringing wet and in no position to aimlessly wonder around in this deep canyon - in the dark - risking injury from walking off a cliff - or who knows what. He wouldn't have survived to see the sun rise if he did not have the provisions to build a fire in a snowstorm. Being prepared for the worst saved his life. With hounds the adventure is in the chase!

On the flip side of the coin, I have seen stump sitters melt down when a bear shows up at the bait. There is some real intimidation about a bear coming into you on his terms, in his house; especially if it is getting dark. Many a man was ready to soil himself when he had to leave his tree in the dark while a bear sat close by watching him. This critter can eat you - and now he is holding all of the cards.

We used to bait bears with rejected cookies from cookie manufacturers. The bears would often dig through a bait pile, carefully selecting their favorite cookies. A good friend of mine told me that when leaving his tree stand in the dark, he felt like a giant Oreo cookie with a flashing "eat me" sign on him! It gets the mind thinking; right Todd? You can really test your mettle when you are tracking a wounded bear in the dark - alone! I've had them warn me when I got too close and they did not or could not run, but weren't ready to cash it in yet either. A leopard, lion, buffalo or elephant would have taken me in those cases - without warning!

A bear on the other hand often will growl at you as if to say, "That is close enough buddy!" I once tracked a bear I wounded at last light on my hands and knees in total darkness with a faulty flashlight. I slowly advanced forward crawling along on the ground in an Aspen thicket, checking one leaf at a time for blood. The blood trail was almost non-existent with only blood from the entrance wound occasionally brushing a leaf here or there. A couple hundred yards and several hours later, I crawled within

The INNER FORCE

twenty feet of the fatally wounded bear - unknown to me until he let out a ferocious snarl and beat some trees around him. It was a warning to me to retreat, a warning that one would seldom get from any of the big five in Africa!

I have also seen plenty of cowards, strutting like tom turkeys below a hound-treed bear. How about a bear or cougar scared shitless in a tree, not shitless as in the case where a bear lost bodily functions on my daughter and son-in-law whom stood below the tree. I would be referring to Sara and Chris! Yes, the hunt is over with hounds if you get to the tree, but it just started if you are in the tree. Two different ways. Both good.

"The Meinert gang with a 650 lb bear"

The same fellow who told me real men hunt with hounds also told me he would never hunt a leopard over bait. The only gaming method would be to track it until it charges and then shoot him! This well-educated fool probably would stand in front of a freight

Frank Schmitz

train if he found a pair of tights, a cape, and a shirt with an S on its chest in a phone booth. I believe you should respect life versus play with death. After all, such tactics endanger your companions' welfare as well as your own. Besides, not many men are willing to die for your foolish games.

I prefer spot and stalk hunting or still hunting, although other methods can produce rewarding results, too. Twice on Kodiak Island I cut black tailed buck tracks, tracked them down and killed them. I had snow and good conditions. In both cases I jumped the bucks several times during the day before they wore down enough to give me the shot I needed.

This type of hunting is a test of endurance and stamina. It is not for the weak of heart, but is very gratifying. The bucks try everything to elude you. They will climb high, charge low, circle around and double back. Often you have to study tracks carefully to stay with the right animal. One buck grew so tired under my pursuit that the last several hundred yards I followed him by sound - I could hear him crashing ahead me.

The other buck had bedded under a blown over tree, sure that he eluded me. As I approached, he jumped from is bed, surprising the both of us. A quick and perhaps lucky off-hand shot finished the largest black tail I had ever seen. However, I almost lost him after I shot him. I thought I saw him tipping over in my scope as I reloaded. The next instant the buck was gone. Moving to where he stood when I took the shot, to my surprise his track continued on in the fresh snow. As I followed his track, a mockingbird screamed out from a bush eighty yards below me on the steep mountainside. At first I ignored the birds cries as I followed the track. I kept replaying the shot in my mind and was sure I had seen the buck start to fall. How could his track continue on?

I went back to the place of the shot and realized another track had intersected the trail. The buck had fallen through a bush, knocking fresh snow to the ground. The snow had covered his fall imprint. There, descending from the bush was a skid mark in the snow. It was like a toboggan run leading down the steep mountainside. The buck lay under the bush where the magpie was still calling . The bird was waiting for me to begin the gutting out duties so it could enjoy a free meal.

I learned a lesson from that experience - never ignore what the other animals of the forest are telling you. That bird was calling me to my kill, just as a squirrel will rat you out while making a stalk.

Speaking of morphadite improvisions, on that hunt the first day out partner Dave Bley and I were stalking a black tail in a heavy snowstorm. We struggled to keep our scopes clear and twice I blew snow from my magniported barrel. I shot my first black tail and we hurried to skin and quarter it and pack it to the beach before dark. We had followed the tracks of a giant Kodiak bear as we hunted this deer, so we could not help thinking that my shot may have rung the dinner bell - signaling him to return for a free meal.

Back in camp that evening, Dave volunteered to wipe my gun down with oil to protect it from the saltwater conditions we were hunting in.

Shortly he asked, "What kind of gun barrel is this?

I responded "It's just magniported to reduce re-coil."

"Well why do they make the barrel circle out like this?" he asked.

"What are you talking about. All barrels are circular!" I responded.

"Not like this, it mushrooms out and back in"!

"Holy Mollie!" I realized ice must have built up in my barrel causing it to blow up when I shot the buck. It looked like an acorn had been stuffed into it. Now what! It's the beginning of the hunt, we can shoot four deer each, and my barrel is blown up!

The light bulb blinks on. I ask the camp cook, Scooby, " Do you have a hack saw around hear?"

"Sure!" Scooby says. He went and fetched one for me. "What do you want with a hack saw anyway?"

"Well its an old tradition where I grew up that every time you kill something, you saw your barrel off an inch!" I replied.

Haha, "Right!" Scooby laughs until the hardened teeth of the saw started to cut across my barrel. Then his eyes lit up as he screamed, "Frank stop, that! It will ruin your gun!"

Well, the barrel was sawed off and the last two bucks I told the story to were shot with my sawed off seven mag. In fact, I hunted several years with the gun before getting a new barrel.

Another improvised hunting method that sometimes works is after jumping an animal or blowing the stalk, is simply running after it.

Frank Schmitz

One time I blew a stalk on a pair of huge couse deer bucks when the wind shifted, taking my scent to their noses.

My guide and I ran after them to the next ridge where we spotted one of the bucks clearing the top of the following ridge. Again we ran to that ridge only to see him clear yet another ridge at the last second. We ran to that ridge as darkness was overtaking the mountains. We searched the opposite mountainside with our spotting scopes until we located the buck. Thinking that he was two drainages removed from us, he calmly rested in his bed under a pin oak. As last light darkened my scope, I shot and killed this record book buck in his bed from 350 yards away. When hunting - be flexible, improvise, but never quit. Sometimes the animal wins on the first several encounters, but stay with him, keep searching, make your own magic!

Back in Africa we are still looking for the sable. It's tracks become muddled. We spread out looking at the ground, searching for sign. I'm moving along when I noticed that everybody has stopped in mid-stride, as if instantly frozen. I freeze too. Our eyes scan the bush around us. There are boulder size shadows in the bush; one slowly swaggers. We have accidentally walked right into the center of a half-dozen daydreaming and dozing elephants. The animals become uneasy as our scent fills the air. They start appearing all around us. The elephants were standing motionless in the bush - here all along.

How can you not see a fricken elephant much less a whole damn herd! If a calf gets too close to us we will face the mother's wrath momentarily. If a bull feels like we have threatened his harem we are likely to be stomped to death shortly.

The confused elephants start trumpeting and tramping around nervously. I notice the Grim Reaper and Company are moving backwards in slow motion - as cautious as a herd of stampeding turtles in a hail storm. Jumbos encroach on three sides of us as we make our slow, torturous retreat. One fast move and we could bring the herd stampeding down on us.

Dust swirls and rises in the trees as I see big patches of gray in the shadows of the bush; feet moving, ears flapping, nervous trunks testing the air. Then in one huge motion, all of Africa flashes in front of me - solid motion from ground to sky. A loud trumpet sounds. The earth rocks and rolls in a wild fury and then all are gone. The silence returns.

The INNER FORCE

We look at each other astonished and revitalized with a new injection of adrenaline. Life is good, especially if you are not elephant toe jam! I never did see the big jumbos very clearly; just lots of gray shadows, a foot, an ear and then gone. Even animals that size can disappear in this cover.

Yesterday the lions hit and devoured one of our leopard baits. Double Dick is setting a new bait elsewhere. The leopard that made the earlier strike did not come back. It was a big male and he apparently knew it was a trap. We hope his stomach will win him over in the next few days.

In the evening we cruise the dusty trails trying to figure out where the buffalo went. We walk a few draws looking for spoor; then drive some more. We finally spot some buffalo standing in thick brush right off the trail at dark. We slowing drive by them. Maybe twenty buffalo just watch us. There are no bulls visible, but surely several are in the thick bush behind the herd.

Each time we've pass them, I've hoped that they would run away. I fear we will spot a good bull and Nixon will want me to shoot him. I don't want to shoot a buffalo from the truck. Yet, I don't want to offend Nixon by passing up an easy, safe opportunity either. It is a dilemma for me. Luckily darkness comes and we do not see a good bull.

We stop and cables are hooked from the truck's battery to a spot light. My comrades know there are no rules in Africa. With a spot light we can drive into the bush and find the bulls. But there are still rules to follow - the rules of my heart. This mighty beast deserves respect. I will not kill one like a common poacher.

I speak up. "Nixon my friend, here's the deal. I will not shoot a buffalo this way. I will not shoot a buffalo from a truck, let alone using a spotlight. I do not need a buffalo that badly. If I can't get him by hunting on foot in the bush, so be it. It would make me sick and ruin my entire hunt if I shot him from the truck."

Nixon says okay and relays the message in the African tongue to the others. They go "oh" and it is settled. We slowly drive the dirt trails towards camp. Nixon shines the light and says "Maybe we will see a civet cat or other night creature." Everyone is quiet in the truck, they know we could have ended the quest for a buffalo. Now we will have to do it as hunters!

I wonder what they are thinking but am glad we got that cleared up. The first encounter with buffalo while on foot in the bush had my heart a pumping. It was very exciting. Since then I

Frank Schmitz

have relaxed a little realizing that their will for self-preservation overpowers their will for confrontation.

The loneliness that is building in my heart for my soul mate controls my mind at times. I find myself forgetting that I am buffalo hunting. The powers in a man's loins is a controlling force and find myself reminding this blue-eyed outer body to stay focused, stay ready. I had better not let myself be caught daydreaming in the bush of Africa. Buffalo - his house, his bedroom, you know the saying. frick with the bull and you will get the horn. With this beast you want to be the fricker not the fricky. Well time to wash my mouth out with soap and go to bed.

Oh, I almost forgot. When I was walking to Nixon's house this afternoon, I looked toward the lake. The big croc was back on the sand bar, but this time on the opposite end of it. I only had my camera with me, so I snuck up to within 100 yards, took two pictures of him, and left without disturbing the old dinosaur. They are lime green and much prettier than I expected.

Again, it reminded me of the darn video game. The croc is beating me. He just casually rests on the bank of the lake. It is a truly awesome looking creature. On one hand, the more I mess with them the more I want crocodile boots - but on the other hand, the less I really want to shoot one. This reptile is a killing machine. However, I think if he's made it this long, maybe he deserves to see my grandkids grow up. I think I'll just let it go if I don't get one on my next try. I had my chance anyway.

Frank Schmitz

June 10

I slept like a dead log last night. I went to bed at 8:00 PM because I had nothing to do. I still had no paper to write on to pass the time, nothing to read, and nobody to bullshit with. I felt lonely and bored. I wondered what was going on at home and missed the warm body of my business partner, best friend and wife that has been beside me in bed for nearly all of my adult life. At the crack of dawn this morning we'll go to where the buffalo were last night and see if we can relocate them.

We arrive in the area and take up their spoor, following it through the bush. One time, I felt like we were miles from civilization. Then I heard the distant rumble of a semi-truck going down a road. It reminded me of being in the great north woods of Wisconsin. I often thought I had escaped the road, deep in the forest. Then I'd hear a car in the distance,. the sound echoing in the forest. It would start at my left side and go three quarters the way around me before disappearing back at my left side, leaving me wondering where the road was.

The sound also echoes in the mountains of Idaho where we pack in on horseback to escape the grasp of modern society. We often hear gunshots that sound like they are coming from the drainage we are hunting. In reality, this drainage opens up into yet another drainage across a major river. If a hunter over there shoots with his gun pointed in our direction, the muzzle blast carries for miles.

Another example is sitting on a distant mountaintop. Then "braaashrooomm," a jet flies over. Or, you look into the wonders of the heavens at night and a damn satellite buzzes past. You cannot completely escape anymore.

We all have preconceived ideas of how a different place, especially a foreign land should be. Most people imagine Africa as a vast, open undeveloped country filled with wild animals, loin clothed men, and bare breasted women. But the 1800's are long gone. Cape Town has skyscrapers, brick paved streets and fancy restaurants. If you were sitting in a bar in Cape Town looking out the window and had to guess where you were, New York and Paris would be considered before Cape Town, Africa. Yet, it'is surrounded by poverty-stricken shantytowns.

Frank Schmitz

Zimbabwe's Harare has a poor, third-world city appearance about it, but that does not mean they don't have highways, cars, trains, factories, and other ingredients of modern day life. The people who occasionally get to see television and all the wonders of modern America have their own misconceptions of how life is in America. For example, when asked I tell the locals I live in Idaho which is located in the Western mountains. I explain the area is rather remote and I have twenty plus horses, dogs, cats, goats, chickens and other farm animals.

With a puzzled look they state, "Idaho? Where is Idaho"?
I respond, "In the Western part of the USA!"
"Oh, the West! Do you have horses?"
"Yes,". I reply
"Do you see Indians?"
"Well, yes the Indians are still around!"
They will look at me and ask, "Did you ever kill an Indian?"
I say, "No, then I would be in prison."
"What? Well, do you see many"?

I explain that I do see them, but not in loin cloths and head dresses like they envision. If I tell them I was born in Wisconsin they will ask what city is near. I'll say Milwaukee, but most times they just look puzzled. Then I add that the next largest city is Chicago. A smile will often come to their face as they say, "Chicago- bang, bang, bang, bang - Chicago," imitating a mobster holding a machine gun. It shows how history remains with a place for a long time.

Anyway, we follow the spoor. It drops into a drainage, then a dry creek bottom. We follow it to where the herd's going. They were going to water to drink - right across from camp! As I slept like a dead log, the buffalo had come to me, come to camp. Damn these beasts! The noise of our awaking camp had driven them off.

We follow the spoor back up into the bush away from camp. The wind is good as we follow their tracks for an hour. They split up in the heavy grass. The tracks are lost. We pick our way forward, finding random signs of them. Fresh crap, a broken branch, a track here or there, and then the brush crackles in front of me. I look up to see a giraffe that had been watching us run off. When they run their long legs and necks rock back and forth. It looks like slow motion. Even with their strange gait they cover ground quickly. Very animated and a sight to behold.

The INNER FORCE

I watched the big creature disappear into the bush and notice black shadows in the bush where the giraffe has gone. A quick confirmation with my binoculars tells me it is the buffalo. Nixon and I duck down, signaling to Bones and Gravedigger to stay put. We crawl forward in the grass until we are within fifty yards of them. We peak up and study them. I can see maybe a dozen shadows in the thick bush around us. Nixon examines them carefully as twenty minutes pass by.

When I started hunting, my first close encounters with wild game invigorated me. A couple times I found myself tracking wounded bears in the dark. Sometimes they would start growling to let me know I was close enough - exciting! I had a Russian Boar come back to life on me once just as I was going to start gutting it. His big ugly snapping jaws met the muzzle of my 357 at point blank range, less than two feet from my face. That gets the old ticker going.

Danger is something one should not go looking for, but if it comes your way, it is how you respond to it that frequently separates the survivors from the deceased. If you freeze or panic, you are a victim of whatever is evolving around you. If you feel no fear, you can respond or react to the situation. It is the ability to kiss the ugly face of death on the check instead of running for your life that will save you.

I had several brushes with disaster in my earlier occupation as a builder and contractor. Three different construction accidents on scaffolding almost took me out. I had to jump for it or react to the collapsing structure to see another day. I fell from eighteen, twenty-four and thirty-six feet and walked away all three times. The most serious injury I sustained was breaking several ribs when I rode out and jumped from twenty-four feet as the scaffolding gave way. When you are subjected to a life threatening situation you either panic or respond. I have always responded. When free-falling from any substantial distance there is a terrific rush of adrenaline that can make time stand still. (Or so it seems.)

These falls always seemed slow - to last forever - even if they lasted mere seconds. You could think, decide what to do, and respond, all in that short time frame. The adrenalin rush enables you to think at ten. if not one hundred times your normal rate. When your mind moves into hyper speed your thoughts are so rapid it makes everything around you seem like it is in slow motion. Sometimes it almost comes to a standstill. This is why people

Frank Schmitz

say "their life flashed before their eyes." The adrenaline filled mind thinking at one hundred times its normal rate can think, analyze and reflect on lots of things in seconds. It is a feeling of time almost standing still; if you do not panic you can react to the situation and save yourself.

I remember floating toward earth along with concrete block and clay flue tiles gently floating to the ground around me as I maneuvered myself to land on my hands and knees. However, I did not think my brother-in-law, Steve, was maneuvering to land on my back like he was going for a horsy ride, but it happened. Both of us came away uninjured.

Another time I slipped off the scaffolding thirty-six feet from the ground like a nuclear warhead. I was able to aim myself towards a roof overhang halfway down. I remember thinking that I had to turn my shoulder inward while tucking my head up so that I would hit with the upper back portion of my shoulder instead of my head. I was able accomplish this as planned, thus breaking my fall. The rest of the way down I was able to turn and land on my feet - without breaking my legs! The whole time I was falling I was thinking, watching and picking landing spots. After crashing to the ground, I stood up and walked into the building where several shocked people stood looking at me.

They stuttered out, "Where did you come from?" I responded that I had just fallen off the top of the building. Then the post-adrenaline rush seized me. My legs began to shake uncontrollably as I said, "I think I need to sit down." I left some shoulder skin on the roof, but other than that I was okay. I was able to respond because adrenaline allows you to think rapidly, not because I am graceful or acrobatic. Hell, I can't scratch my ear and pick up my feet at the same time.

My first encounter with time standing nearly still was when I was between ten and eleven years old. My older brother, Mike, and I were having a tree-climbing contest in our front yard. The object of our attention was a two and one-half story tall maple tree. Eventually we reached the spindly thin top of the main trunk. I reached for the highest branch when the small branch I was standing on gave way. I still wonder how I fell through the tree without hitting other branches. I remember thinking that I had to catch a branch or I would break my legs when I hit the ground. I was able to grab the last branch in the tree for only a split-second, but it apparently broke my fall enough so that I hit

The INNER FORCE

the ground unhurt. My younger brother, Jeff, was running for the house screaming and thinking I must be dead. Sure, when I got up I was shaking like a shackled slave on castration day, but I was not injured. After that I often dreamed of falling from things and landing safely. Subconsciously I knew I could do it and come out okay.

So if I do not live to tell the story of my encounter with the leopard, buffalo or some other beast, you will know that either my gun failed me or the shot did not stop the attack! However, rest assured I had time to think and make my peace....that I was not scared but accepted the honorable quick death that fate had planned for me.... and that I'm resting in a better place where I will patiently wait for just a flicker of eternity for my wife to join me.

The wind is very good, right in our faces. The buffaloes mingled, completely unaware of us crouching in the grass. Then Nixon says, "There he is. There is the bull. Get up, rest on this bush and shoot him." I look through my scope into an opening in the bush. I see wide thick bosses, the heavy upper portion of a buffalo bull's horns. I see his massive head, but his body is just a black shadow camouflaged with the bush. I realize a Cape buffalo is probably the only animal on earth capable of killing you after it'is dead. Even with a heart shot, the momentum of the charging buffalo could still steamroll over you like a runaway eighteen wheeler on a mountainside!

Nixon is whispering to me from my left to take him through the shoulder. I draw a mental picture of where shoulders and bone structure would be in the black silhouette. I lower the cross hairs to that location. The trigger is squeezed, the report of the .416 kicks into my shoulder and the 400 grain hollow point is propelled into the mighty beast. The first shot slams into the beast is paramount, with the force of a Kansas tornado hitting a farm house. He is visually rocked. His legs quiver back and forth buckling. He appears to be going down.

I eject the shell and work the bolt forward solidly jamming the next round half-in half-out. We are definitely not in the Land of Oz, but in a rapidly real and deteriorating situation. I am struggling with the weapon to free the jammed round and chamber it. Although perhaps only a split second, I finally clear the shell and slam the bolt on the next round.

Frank Schmitz

    Although only a split second has gone by, I look up to see the bull is running broadside to my right. This part I do not remember, but I pull up and shoot instinctively. I do not remember aiming or pulling the trigger, but later realized this shot hit him high in his right front shoulder.

    This shot got his attention. This shot made him realize where the attack was coming from. It made him understand that he had been challenged to a duel to the death. The bull was willing to meet this challenge. Without hesitating while in full stride , he swung his head towards me and his 2,000 pounds of muscle and mass followed his head. This is when. The charge began. I felt like a stalled UPS truck parked on the tracks with a freight train barreling down at me at 70 mph. The mail was definitely about to be delivered.

    This is what I remember vividly; his eyes met mine; when the blue-eyed one connected with the dark eyes of the enraged bull. There were no whites in his eyes but- just bright red. I could see the fires of hell in his eyes. They were filled with hate and for a very justifiable reason seeing as I had just waged war upon him. The second shot was supposed to be delivering the wrath of the devil to him. But instead it merely enraged the powerful beast, changing the ominous stare of his eyes as they turned to the raging fires of hell! He had turned the tables on me, as he directed his power, hate and wrath upon me in an inevitable charge.

The INNER FORCE

The bull was coming for me at forty yards...a distance he could cover in less than three and one-half, maybe four seconds. At that moment, the blue-eyed one stood there with his gun at his side with the bolt open; the spent cartridge laying on the ground, chamber empty; and the third and final round tucked in the magazine waiting for its orders, waiting to be called to service.

This is when I had the adrenaline rush you only get when your life is in eminent danger. The blood coursing through my arteries, filling my brain with oxygen; clearing my mind of everything else in this world. For those who have been here understand how at times like this unfold and your brain starts to function at ten or fifty times its normal rate. The power of your mind makes the world stand still. What is happening around you begins to transpire in slow motion. I have been here before, only floating to the ground with concrete block floating around me as I am thinking at what seems like a normal rate but indeed is at light speed.

Frank Schmitz

I see the bull coming as I raise my gun. This unfamiliar weapon must now be an extension of my body, my mind and my soul. I feel the bolt grab the last round as it slides smoothly into the chamber. The bolt locking down behind it. The bull is at thirty yards now. We are separated by two maybe three seconds of time. This beast is like a nuclear warhead speeding towards my ship. A freight train barreling down the tracks to which I am tied. It is a time when panic or fear means almost certainly either injury or death. My mind speaks to me, "Take your time. There is still plenty of time. Aim carefully. You have to brain him. It is your only shot."

The gun's stock is on my shoulder as my eye comes to the scope. The bull is now at twenty yards, one or two seconds of this game still remaining. My cross hairs bear down between his eyes below his bosses. I see sweat spraying from the right side of his head. He is at ten yards when my brain sends the message to my right index finger. It is time, shoot now! As I'm about to pull the trigger his head dodges out of my scope. SHIT! I pull down trying to get him back in the scope. There is no time for fear, but I now think that I have lost this fight. He has out maneuvered me.

It is the classic hook maneuver a bull does on his charge; duck and swing, impale his aggressor, send him airborne over his back, and then turn to stomp him to death. I struggle desperately to bring my crosshairs back to his head. In this adrenaline-hyped twilight zone, my rifle swings swiftly - yet slowly - as its visual picture re-centers on the mighty buffalo's head. His massive "warhead" slowly brushes across the surface of the African dirt, dust swirling up from the ground as he skids towards me.

The fire of hell is gone from his eyes and he no longer is capable of the deadly hook maneuver. The big beast lies seven or eight yards from me. My own eye still looking through my scope, finally centered on his brain bucket. I stand there aiming ready to shoot not knowing if time is standing still or if the mighty beast is dead. I hold my final shot in case the second spirit brings him back to his feet.

I realize the rest of the world is still moving. Time is marching on. The bull's spirit has been exorcized and he no longer breathes fire. There is a fine line between when life really starts and really stops. Thirty seconds ago, life really started for that bull and thirty seconds later, life really stopped - more so for the Cape buffalo than me!. But I suspect both our spirits returned to normal speed wherever they were.

The INNER FORCE

The bull looks peaceful. Nixon stands to my right. The 375's barrel is smoking its last round in the chamber. I do not remember hearing the report of his gun, but he had shot the bull twice. When I thought I had seen sweat spraying off the bull's head, it was really blood tracing out the path of Nixon's exiting bullet.

The world moves back into full speed, my heart is pounding with excitement as I look at Nixon and he looks at me. We smile proudly at each other.

Nixon says, "Shit Frank, I thought he was going to get you for a minute there. You killed him on the first shot but he did not know it, did he?"

"Neither did I. Good shooting my friend. Thank you." We shake hands and laugh; we are alive and are on the top of the world. We stand tall on the top rung of the ladder known as the food chain. It is good to be in the company of a real man, a professional. I learned long ago it is more important to be a professional, than an expert. A professional offers professional advice or service based on experience in the field. An expert offers expert opinion learned in a book, in a classroom without hands-on experience. Expert opinion verses professional advice.

Frank Schmitz

Remember the definition of an expert. X is a mathematical symbol for an unknown quantity and spert is a drip under pressure. With that said, you pick your poison!

Today I have come, seen and conquered. Today Mother Nature embraced me and holds me tight to her tender bosom. I hold her back, cherishing her love and companionship, but I know the bitch she can be. I have seen her dark side and know how she will cast you aside in the blink of an eye! But, today I wallow in her warmth enjoying the sweet taste of victory. Today the bitch is mine. I have had my way with her. I have felt her comfort, tasted her sweetness, heard my prayers being answered and seen the light. I had better cherish the moment because tomorrow is another day and perhaps it may not be my day next time!

The buffalo is a good buffalo. People who measure a trophy with a tape measure want a buffalo 40" or more. I will not insult this great beast by stretching a tape to his horns. Just like we have not measured any of the others on this trip. This animal died honorably. He is mine and that is that!

I suddenly feel something warm running down the side of my neck. I touch it with my hand. It is blood. I realize somewhere along the way a spiked thorn bush branch must have hooked into my ear. The thorns ripping it open enough that I may wear a scar on that ear for the rest of my life. As the blood pours freely I realize it would be a dignified tattoo if it heals that way.

I walk up to the big Cape buffalo and admire him. Suddenly he gasps, lifting up his head slightly as if coming back to life. Then his head falls back to the ground. The second spirit has left him. He will wait for me in the life after, so as to wage war again. Good riddens my friend - until that time!

I kneel down beside this beast that challenged my life and rub my hands across his massive bosses down the sweeping horn to its dark inward pointing tips. I lay my hand on his forehead, feeling his course hair caked with dirt. I feel his power and admire his mass. The buffalo is huge, only surpassed by the gigantic giraffe I harvested days ago. He surely weighs a ton. Again I hope there is a happy hunting ground, and hope we will meet again to duel in mother natures way!

For now we all rejoice in the sweet taste of victory. In front of us lies the big job of reducing this magnificent creation of our makers into life sustaining cuts of protein to feed the families of our comrades. Transporting this mass of muscle and bone back

The INNER FORCE

to camp is no small task. Loading this massive beast onto our Land Rover is a team effort, requiring everybody's participation. Every human's hands and legs are required to try and hoist this mammoth beast up into the back of the truck. It is an effort of song and physical force that coordinates our struggle.

Nixon unites this physical endeavor by leading with an old customary chant that would be similar to Heave-HO. This song goes more to the tune of, "Hoggla Majunga, Huggla Majunga, Hoooo!" We all lift and hold. The chanting song continues over and over again until the seemingly impossible is achieved - a remarkable collaborative effort, coordinated by an historic ritual. That was an inspirational experience by itself. An example of team spirit and unity one could only experience in the Dark Continent.

In the afternoon we spot a big croc again. We estimate him to be 150 yards away if I can sneak to the shoreline. He is sunning himself on a sandbar off shore. I make the stalk to the shoreline and get a comfortable rest. I have the 375 and know the gun will do nothing unless I brain him or break his spin. I estimate the location of his brain behind his left eye. I figure the 300 grain bullet will be dropping a little at 150 yards, so I hold a little high. Boom! The bullet sails just over his head. The croc dives into the drink.

Frank Schmitz

We wade to the sand bar to check for sure. There is no indication of a hit, but we wait an hour and an half just to be sure. It would take a while for the gases in his stomach to bloat him if he would have been brained and flopped into the lake,. He would then float to the top, like a twelve foot leather bobber.

Dixon asks, "How did you hold? That gun shoots a little high." Well, if I held high and the gun shoots high, then for sure that shot was high. We pace off the distance. It is 100 yards rather than 150 yards. Oh well...that is why you should bring your own gun and know how it shoots. We have three bullets left for the .416 and a half box of the ineffective solids for the 375. The only thing I will shoot at is a leopard - given the chance.

If I had my 7 mag I would have, without a doubt, blasted holes in this beady-eyed tooth holder. I also would have let the air out of a monster bushbuck and probably a duiker and a baboon. The weapons I'm using are just too much gun. They cannot thread the

The INNER FORCE

needle like the trusty 7 mm. I have forty rounds for my 7 mm and only three for the .416. Too bad nobody around here owns a 7 mag that I could borrow for a week.

It has been two weeks since I had any hard booze. Tonight I have the urge for some whiskey to celebrate the buffalo hunt. They had somebody go to town and get me a new note pad to keep me from being too bored and a bottle of scotch whiskey, whatever that is. It sounds too expensive, but is very smooth with not much bite. I had only two drinks because you cannot celebrate too much by yourself. Nixon and Dixon joined me for one and then went to take care of their business. It gave me a chance to catch up on three days of scribbling. I turned the candle off at midnight - after having had the chance to relive one of the most exciting days of my life - several times!

Frank Schmitz

June 11

We spent the morning chasing crocs around, but only saw one big one that we could not get close to. I think these guys have wised up.

There was a strike on the leopard bait at Malarat Camp so we will head out at midday for another ritual in the blind. It will be a long day...I am sure a long bad-ass day or night in a blind.

On the way I wanted to take pictures of local people, their homes and so forth. I figured the people would be offended if I took their picture, maybe feeling inferior because of their poverty-stricken lives. I was amazed that Nixon was proud to have pictures taken of the new house he is building!

"You taking pictures of my house!"

"Yes," I say.

"Take one from the front. Get the builder in!" The builder and laborer scamper to the top of a pile of mason sand and proudly hold up their arms, trowels in hand for the picture. Having done masonry work for most of my life, I found the solid wall masonry construction of Nixon's house very interesting. I explained to Nixon that I was a mason and owned my own business for twenty years before becoming an outfitter. He could not understand that I would actually do manual labor.

"Oh, you own a big building company!" he responds.

"No, I had a small company and would do this work in the field every day." I explained.

Nixon frowns and looks at me, the concept is too foreign to him - that a common laborer, a man that works with his hands could be hunting in Africa. He is sure I am a wealthy aristocrat from a land where all white men are rich!

Later I see some women sitting on logs in front of their meager huts. They notice the camera aimed their way. Instantly they start waving. "Take my picture. Take my picture," they insist. Even a woman with her breast exposed feeding her infant wants me to photograph her. They are obviously proud of themselves and what they have. That is good. Very good because it means that they know their lives are getting better,. and they feel good about themselves.

Frank Schmitz

We arrive at the hunting area and are met by Double Dick and his staff assistants. He says to me, "Good day, Sir! Tonight you will be very happy I am sure. We have a very nice leopard hitting the bait."

"That is wonderful," I reply, but I can not say I share his confidence. My memory of the long wait several nights earlier is fresh in my mind and I expect an agonizing ass stretching tonight. As stated before, my personal capability of sitting for any extended period of time is very limited. Having always been very active, I am either doing something or sleeping. Neither action is conducive to a sitting angle.

The blind is another work of art. The bait looks good. Everything well planned as always. We settle into the blind and Nixon asks if he can back me up tonight. We are very close to the National Park boundary. If the leopard gets into the park he is gone. We cannot go in after him, so we must make sure we finish him off. I say, "Sure you're the boss, Nixon."

We settle in, the .416 resting through a tiny hole in the blind and the 375 next to me. Tonight Dixon (Bones) is in the blind, too. He will work the spotlight if needed. I think to myself, "Wouldn't it be nice if a leopard would show up before total darkness?"

Several hours of daylight pass and darkness engulfs us. Stars shine brightly overhead as we silently wait. I look for the big dipper and see a weird circular constellation of stars. I think to myself, "I don't remember seeing that constellation before. I realize that I have not gazed into the night sky of the southern hemisphere very often before.

I continue to sit, trying not to move, peeking through the tiny hole my gun balances in. Nothing but total darkness. Visibility zero. I watch and 'stare' with my ears trying to 'see' each sound. I imagine a leopard prowling in silently, smelling, and looking. You know the cat has to feel something is not right, but his stomach leads him on. I wonder if one is close by - standing in the blackness at an arms length like the other night. We wait.

When hunting dangerous game in Africa, wise men have backups and allow them to shoot. It is not a time for macho pride. It is not a time for saying I want it my way or the highway. We all have dreams of wild adventures....adventures that truly challenge you.

Not like the stupid reality show everyone is watching on television. "Survivor." It is so ridiculous because everybody thinks these people are suffering and in some sort of peril while every safety net possible is in place. A helicopter with all the finest medicine and doctors would be there in a heartbeat if someone would get hurt. However, if you go looking for danger in the real world you are liable to find it. And sometimes stupidity is paid for with lives, human lives that is!

When things go wrong in the backcountry - you get left out, caught in bad weather or injured - you have to account for yourself. It's simple. If you can't, you are done. The wilderness is not a game. In many of the places cell phones do not work. And if they did, nobody would know where you were calling from anyway.

We have disillusioned city folk come to our lodge in Idaho wanting to ride in the backcountry, white water raft, mountain bike or climb. They want wilderness adventure, but if a bug bites them in the ass the world has to come to a screeching halt. They are scared stiff if they see a bear or mountain lion. I sleep outside in a tent or under the stars at least three months of the year. But these guys, one night out and they turn religious.

I had a group of eight city slickers staying overnight in our backcountry cabin, The Gilmore Ranch. The horses I have there need salt and minerals so there's a mineral lick just outside of the front door. But the game likes it too. Deer or elk will come

Frank Schmitz

in camp at dark, going to the lick. That night a cow and calf elk were at the lick.

It was ninety percent dark and this one older fella wanted to show off what a tough guy he was to his grandchildren. So he decided to go outside and scare the elk. The elk are naturally fearful of man. They'll run when they see you. A minute later he comes charging back through the door. The poor super hero is white as a ghost. His eyes bulge wide, he gasps - out of breath, and he stutters that there is the most horrific mortifying beast out there. It is huge and started coming towards him!

I think that the poor shocked fella must have run into a moose and go out to take a look. There is my big black mule, Rosie. She is wondering if we have any treats she could lick out of our hands. Tough guys like this should not be looking for high adventure in the wilderness. They should stick to knitting and crocheting!

Anyway, in the real wilderness a backup man or plan can prevent an injury or save a life - and/or injury. Tonight on this leopard hunt, the very reason that Nixon has asked if he can back me up. He explains that we are extremely close to the National Park boundary and if a leopard shows after dark a quick clean kill would be nice, but most of all we do not want the leopard to escape into the park. I agree. If a leopard shows lets put the shit to him. We had enough extra curricular activity with the Cape buffalo.

Double Dick said it was a big tom cat that hit this bait last night. The leopard that hit the first bait we hunted was medium size and had not returned. This is the one we want. The moon phase remains the same. No moon. No wind. No noise. Total darkness. Visibility is zero while in the blind! I cannot make out a shadow - nothing.

I could hardly breathe or twitch for fear it would be heard. We sat totally motionless even as a severe pain from not moving sent shockwaves from my buttocks up my back.

As I sit here my mind drifts to a mountaintop in New Zealand. We had spent six hours scaling a cold, snow covered mountainside wondering if the animal we were after would be up there. The creature we hunt resides at 12,000 feet above sea level. The greatest challenge of this hunt is to be physically able to climb the rugged cliffs to this altitude. - to get to the top of the world in order to succeed.

The INNER FORCE

As we scaled the last rock, there they were. Brown, ghostly figures with long flowing manes like that of an African lion. Thick, short, curved horns adorned their heads. One herd bull with sixteen nannies. My shot rips threw him, hitting a slab of rock on his off side. The confused beast turns and charges me. Bad decision. The next round topples the trophy Himalayan Thar.

I ponder how hunting opportunities vary. A cold snow covered mountaintop at high altitude - fighting weather, thin air and a near vertical landscape - verses flat, warm country trying to be motionless in the dark.

My mind drifts back to pleasant memories of a former trip to Africa. We are sitting on wooden chairs on a stone-laid patio. There are cold Castle beers in our hands and a roaring fire in the nearby fireplace. Crickets chirp their love songs as the stars shine from above. On the fire cooks fresh eland steaks. Latter, our bellies full of tender fillets and cold beer, we decide to go springhare hunting.

Springhares are Africa's version of jackrabbits they are quite similar looking and stand up on their hind hunches like North American rabbits but often they take off hopping like a wallaby or kangaroo.

Frank Schmitz

It is 11 PM when we load up into a Land Rover with shotguns, spotlights and a greyhound dog. Soon we are rip-roaring threw the open fields of grass, the spot light scanning in front of us. Springhares hop up like miniature kangaroos; zipping, zigging and zagging at warp speed. We try to blast them with our shotguns in spite of the fact that we can't really take aim because we're bouncing around wildly in the back of the rig.

At the sound of the gun the greyhound bolts from the truck and a true dog race is on. The track is undefined but the rabbit is real. Put your money down! Sometimes the dog wins; other times the rabbit wins; and once in a while we actually shoot one. By morning we had a dozen springhare.

There was a young boy with us - the houndsman. He was about sixteen years of age. He would have to retrieve the greyhound after the chase. It was hilarious watching the boy chasing the dog chasing the rabbit. It was one of those times that you would have had to be there.

Kind of like when Kyle Sterkenburg told me of his outdoor caper. He and his buddies were out hunting one cold winter morning when Mother Nature came a calling. Kyle was dressed in an insulated, hooded coverall. He scurried off into the forest to do his obligatory duties. You can imagine the struggle of getting out of the heavy coveralls to squat in the cold and snow. After the mission was accomplished he re-dressed and joined up with his waiting buddies.

"Oh boy that was cold!" Kyle stuttered out.

"I have to warm up," he stated, flipping his hood up over his head. And warm up he did as a pile of fresh warm crap from inside his hood landed on his head. I guess you just had to be there!

Back to this night...this hunt is much different.

We've settled into our monotonous state of boredom; click, click, click - three seconds. Like the other night, seconds drag to minutes and minutes to hours.

Several uneventful hours had passed when I heard the first noise; some padding around, then a low chuckling purr, then strong claws against bark as the big cat climbs the tree to the half rotten meat. We can hear flesh being ripped from the hindquarter, teeth popping and more flesh being torn away.

Nixon taps me. It is the signal to prepare to shoot. Dixon turns on the spotlight. As my eyes adjust from total darkness to the light, the most magnificent sight I have ever seen appears before me. A big beautiful cat standing broadside on a limb. His body looks a ghostly light gray with shadowy spots. The spotlight makes it look like a black and white photo. He looks more like an Asian snow leopard than a golden African leopard.

His well-defined, muscular body makes it easy to see his front shoulder. My cross hairs quickly rest on them as the gun fires. Almost simultaneously the 375 fires. Two slugs plow into the big cat. 700 grains of bullet hitting him with the force of Muhammad Ali in his prime. Float like a butterfly. Sting like a bee. The cat crashes to the ground. As quickly as I can reload, he is gone. Minutes later I hear growling, deep angry growls, maybe six or

Frank Schmitz

seven and then the night is dead calm. Five or ten minutes go by before I hear a deep guttural throaty gasp. It is a sound that I have heard often before - the last breath.

I know now he is dead, but Nixon and Dixon remain on high alert. They radio the truck. A couple of minutes later Double Dick arrives with his rig. Nixon orders us into the truck. We load up in the front and back. With two spotlights we drive to the tree. We look for blood from the safety of the truck. There is blood. We follow it by truck for thirty yards until it's near the dirt road that separates the park from the hunting concession. We don't see any more blood, but what we had seen was bright red and bubbly; lung blood. We see no tracks across the dusty road. Remaining in the truck and using spotlights, we search the immediate area. The goal is to find the dead cat or shine his eyes so we can finish him off. Two hours later we decide to head for camp until the morning.

As we leave I say to Nixon, "The cat is dead, don't you think?" He asks me what I think. I'm a little discouraged that we did not recover him now. I was 98 percent sure he was dead. Now I'm 90 percent sure. Look at the facts. We had heard him roaring. We had a perfect broadside shot. We both shot him with powerful weapons. We found blood that indicated a lung hit. We heard the last breath. Nixon says, "You are right; he is dead," as we drive back to camp.

It's after midnight (12:45 AM if I remember right) when I crawled in. We want to leave to go back by 6:00 AM so we sleep fast and hard!

June 12

It's 6:00 AM and we are off to the races. The recent weather has been sunny and dry and each night is warmer. Indian summer I guess. Nixon explains that the reason we did not search harder for the cat last night is because a wounded leopard is one of the most dangerous animals in the world. Taking any chances in the dark is crazy,

I reply, "I understand."

He continues, "We find him this morning. Don't you think?"

"Yes," I respond. "I am confident he's finished!"

Nixon carries on, "Four years ago I have this hunter, and his picture is in our brochures with his leopard. Well, his leopard comes in and he shots it, but it leaves the tree. We drive over there to take a look. There is a spoor, but no leopard. We shine around - no eyes glaring in the darkness. We think he is gone or dead so we get out and are examining the blood. The next thing I know there is a shadow coming, the man screams and I turn. The man is right next to me. The leopard is jumping for him. I pull my gun up and shoot the cat right next to him, just three feet away. The man was crying. I am telling you he just sits down and was crying like a baby. After that no more chances."

The ride to camp seems longer than before and I replay everything in my mind. I think D.D. will have the leopard by the time we get there. Every time I close my eyes, I see the majestic beast standing in the tree looking at me. The vision is burned into my mind.

We turn onto the last stretch of road, the road that leads to the hunting concession and National Park.

Then Nixon speaks again. "We may have a problem, but we will see." I think aloud, "A problem? What kind of problem?"

"Well you know why I wanted to back you up. We did not want the leopard to get into the park, right? The last spoor was near the dirt road. The boundary, right? Well we cannot go into the park!"

"Not even to retrieve a dead animal?" I ask.

"Well, we will see. Here is the problem. We cannot take guns in the park. If the leopard made it past the tall grass into the thick bush it is too dangerous to follow unarmed. The other problem is we do not want to get caught by the border patrol in the park."

I'm thinking it could jeopardize their outfitting license - fine, embarrassment, possible loss of guns, etc.

Nixon continues, "The Border Patrol does not mess around. It is their job to protect the park from poachers; you know poachers are a problem. The Border Patrol is armed with fully automatic weapons. If they see poachers they have the authority to shoot to kill and they do because they do not know if the poachers will shoot back. You see we would not want to be mistaken in our intent."

My heart sinks. I'm worried that I had the life long dream to hunt the great cats; a lifetime of waiting; and now this. We turn into the concession and drive to the bait. D.D. is waiting for us. I hope that his face will stretch into a wide smile when he sees me.

The first indication of bad news is his expression. He looks sober as we pull up. He starts blabbering in Shona, their native tongue. This is the one thing I hate the most. These guys are always talking in Shona so I never know what is going on for sure. D.D. hands me my bullet. After passing through the leopard it lodged into a limb. He has found the spoor...the leopard has crossed the road into the park. Our worst fears are realized.

Now we have to honor the rules of man instead of nature. It is their laws that result in me having to leave the great tom lay were he is. We discuss the situation; it is legal to walk in the park, so unarmed, we decide to trail the spoor into the tall grass for a while. We follow it fifty yards to where the cat had stood the night before. There is a puddle of blood. It is the spot we were looking for; the first spot he stopped. We had hoped that this would be his final resting location, but now we realize that the shot could not have been clean. If he was double lunged, he would have died here. Instead he moved forth into the thick bush. This means he could still be alive and capable of trying to defend himself. This means there is hope that he survives. A hope every hunter prays for if he cannot recover his quarry.

The INNER FORCE

But in my heart, I am sure he did not live. If this is meant to be his final resting place, then that is the fate of destiny. I understand that in nature nothing is ever wasted. He will melt into the natural life and death cycle. Within two or three days the carcass will be nothing but clean bones. It will mean that other predators - perhaps lions, hyenas, and jackals will feast. It means they will not kill something else to feed themselves. It means that one lucky dicker or kudu or some other predator of the grass will survive to mate and bear young. It also means the other forty animals this leopard would have killed to sustain himself until the end of this year will survive. They too will bear young. It means that the pendulum in the balances of nature has swung slightly towards the few animals that prey on vegetation.

In the areas I've hunted outside the park, the grass is thin. It is chewed and grazed back; plains game is abundant because predators are few. We would see lots of many species of antelope every day. Here in the refuge of the park, predator numbers are high and plains game numbers are low. As a matter of fact I have not seen a single antelope or any animal of prey whatsoever. As a reflection of this, the grass is long and thick.

In the near future the predators will begin to starve, turn sick, and die off if the imbalance continues. The grass eating plains game animal numbers will rebound and sky rocket until the grass

Frank Schmitz

is gone. Then the predator populations will recover and the cycle will start over again.

I know the leopard will not go to waste, nothing ever does in nature, but I will be haunted for many years by the image engraved in my mind. My leopard, standing in a tree looking at me.

Nixon assures me the game is not over. We still have two days left to hunt. Maybe there will be another strike. And we can still hunt the bait where the first strike took place. It was a smaller cat, maybe a female, but there is a chance that cat will be back. He can see that I am bummed out as he says, "Lets stay here today and hunt the other bait. We can wait all night. Maybe he will come. What do you say?" "Aah, okay, whatever...." I reply.

We return to camp where more communications are made by radio to Chipimbi Camp and base station - wherever that is. A report comes back the crocodiles are sunning on the sand bar, very close to the blind we built. Obviously crocs are not stupid. They saw us leave this morning and know it is a good day to spend on the beach. Nixon says, "Look Frank. Don't worry. We still have time." Let's lie down and rest it could be a long night. So we go off to some of the huts and crash out.

I rest a little, but mostly replay the visions of the night before. After an hour I get up to see what is going on in camp. I hear voices from the radio room and walk over there. A tall, thin older black man dressed in an old tattered looking army green uniform is in the room. He holds a beat-up machine gun in his hands with an attached thirty to fifty round clip. The gun looks like a vintage WW II model. The patch on his shoulder reads Zimbabwe Wildlife and Parks Officers. An inquiry is going on in Shona about our tire tracks and footprints entering the park. He apparently is satisfied with whatever is told to him, but says he will stay at the camp until I leave. While If I spend the night in a blind he will wait at the truck. He will be a witness to whatever happens if I shoot. We agree. I hope he is patient for the night is long.

Later I ask Nixon what was said. He replies an officer is supposed to be present if they have a hunter. I ask where he was last night. Nixon and Dixon look at each other and laugh and Nixon says, "Look my friend, some things you really do not want to know. Okay! Enough said."

Being human we can never accept things for what they are. We have to analyze and dissect things. We have to formulate reasons and excuses for what has happened. So, I'm thinking....I

The INNER FORCE

have not shot Nixon's guns well. I took only one shot when we sighted in the .416 because we had a limited supply of bullets. The shot was about 3" high at fifty yards. With a 400 grain bullet, I figured that might mean it was dead on or one inch high at 100 yards which is good.

The scope is a German-made Schmidt and Bender and has strange cross-hairs. It has a thin horizontal line through the middle and a heavier vertical line that comes up from the bottom of the optic to the center line. At that point, it turns into a v-shape, ending just above the horizontal line. (This optical site is called a post-uncommon in America. It is the first I have ever seen.) That is the point I was looking at when I sighted it in. Now, before the heat of the moment arrives again I think I have it figured out. If I look at the intersecting points instead of the end of the vertical pin, it will pull my shot down, making it dead on. Last night in the dark I remember seeing the vertical line meeting the horizontal line. In the dark I could not see the V that extended above the horizontal plane. That is where I aimed and shot center of the front shoulder.

I'm thinking this through. If I did not see the top of the vertical pin, the adjustment I would make at the point of the aim would not lower my shot like I was thinking. Instead it would mean I would raise my barrel to adjust, making the shot higher. That is why the leopard escaped a double lung hit! I suddenly realize how this problem escalates even farther.

I come to the conclusion that I have to shoot the gun to reestablish where my zero is before I hunt tonight. Normally that would not sound like a problem at all - would it? Well the problem is I only have two bullets left. If I target shoot one of them I have one bullet left to hunt with. No second shot. No backup shot if we need to follow the most dangerous animal I have ever hunted! The decision is a no-brainer. I have to fire my second to last bullet to establish what my zero is at fifty yards. The adjustment will have to be made without a second shot to confirm its zero, but the shot has to be taken to solidify my mental conscience. I need to satisfy my subconscious that the gun is on, so I can aim and shoot without second guessing or doubting myself. The shot is taken and the adjustment is made.

We only slept about four and one-half hours last night and I am tired. I doze off for about an hour, then lie awake trying to sleep. I have been gone for over a half of a month now and yes,

Frank Schmitz

I am a bit lonely. I miss my wife lots and think of her often. It is understandable that whenever I close my eyes that I think of pussy, but today the pussy is four legged with a ghostly light fur and a spotted coat standing on a limb instead of the furry black triangle a normal mans mind is controlled by. The haunting image will be with me forever, filed along the images of other great beasts that were not meant to be; one of them a vivid image of a huge whitetail I should have had after executing perhaps my best stalk ever, but my rear rifle sight had come loose changing my point of aim. Or, the image burned deep into my mind of when I was a misguided youth...

I had idolized several men, father figures and mentors, listening to their stories of spear fishing and poaching. I have remarkable memories of hound dogging through swamp grass as ring necks pheasants flush into the air in front of me. I am only tall enough to see above the long grass as I watched my hero, my dad, swing his trusty old Browning shotgun "long Tom." It cracks, a bird falls; he swings it again, pow, another one falls. Wow! He's my hero!

Dad and his buddies grew up in a time of plenty and no laws, when a man took whatever he needed from the field. The game laws when they came along were not taken seriously. They just added to the fun. Their cat and mouse games with wardens made for adventure and great stories. They would fondly laugh at these capers.

I thought it was my right of passage, from boy to man, to follow in their footsteps. As a teenager I exercised my American citizen rights of spearing fishing each spring. Carp and suckers were legal game and we speared many. But bass, walleye and northern pike were game fish and closed to spear fishing. Except for spear and release---- into the frying pan! I must admit that was the case on more then a couple of occasions. I never felt guilty about dining on the tender, white meaty fillets.

I pulled my fair share of stunts, but times where changing. Laws were getting stricter. What was acceptable in the good old days would soon be a thing of the past. But I was a bit of a slow learner. One night I decide it was my time for glory as a friend and I set out after a big buck we had seen at dusk. A shotgun and a spotlight were the tools of the night. Being young and easily distracted, we encountered raccoons instead of the trophy swamp

The INNER FORCE

buck that night and I blast away my slugs at them, killing a big old raccoon.

A strange twist of fate greets us as we hiked back to the road, happy with our big old coon. There stands the big buck in some tall swamp grass. He is one hundred yards in front of us, staring into the strange light that shines in his eyes. We look at him for awhile, amazed at his beauty and big rack when all of a sudden the light bulb goes on! Hey I still have one slug in my pocket. The gun is loaded and aimed at his neck. A bolt of fire comes from the barrel and the big boy collapses in the grass. We look at each other with that "holy shit" look on our faces. We did it. Our next thought is let's get the hell out of here!

We run away, never going up to the downed animal. We were afraid someone heard the shot, wardens were converging on us, and we'd wake up in the Crow Bar Hotel looking at a thousand bars and no bartenders! It takes us four hours to build up the nerve to go back. We figure it should be safe by now. We sneak back to collect the big buck, scared shitless the whole time. There is a small pool of blood but no buck when we get to the spot where he had crashed to the ground. I am more relieved than anything that we do not have to continue with our little caper.

Apparently the neck shot grazed him, knocking him out. The deer must have recovered and ran away. Never-the-less, that image haunted me for several years. I could not stand the thought that I may have injured him; and he may have died later, wasting the huge trophy.

It was a blessing in disguise because it quickly cured me of that activity. I never again thought about spotlighting a critter and soon grew up enough to realize my mentors were wrong in their youth. Times are changing and you have to change with them. You need to respect these wild critters. It is a lesson engraved in my mind; all I need to do is think of that night, close my eyes, and I can still see that buck plain as day - even if more than a quarter of a century has come to pass since then.

That night a poacher died and a hunter was reborn. Not that I've never put in an extra tip-up or two since then, but I realized that we have to respect our resources. I haven't been perfect - some laws are just meant to be broken. But flagrant violating or poaching is unacceptable by any measure. I think we should all strive to try to be the best that we can be at everything we do! Along the way we all will falter and slip up occasionally, but that

Frank Schmitz

only will serve as a reminder to try and better ourselves again. So don't kick the guy that is down, just help him up, especially if it's me.

I'm still lying here contemplating how truth is stranger than fiction. I've wait a lifetime to follow my dream of hunting one of the great cats of this world. I put money down five years ago. My finances said 'do not go.' You are an average man playing a rich man's game. I will have to continue to handle bales of hay (that I am allergic to) by hand every day to feed my horses because I put the money on this hunt instead of in a tractor that I really need.

So my time arrives, but my guns do not. Here I am on the opposite side of the world that I call home. Lying in a hut. Waiting for darkness so that I can sit in a blind built of sticks in the company of a stranger with an unfamiliar gun and one bullet. You know how it is when something is haunting you, bothering you, demanding your concentration, forcing you to think it through to its entirety?

Well, this is one of those moments. I know the odds of seeing another leopard is poor - unlikely at best. But I am wondering, can all this be a coincidence that I've come here. My goal is to harvest a leopard. Everything else is frosting on the cake. I end up shooting some animals I never thought about hunting; bush pig, giraffe, and waterbuck. I kill ones that I thought I would if opportunity presented itself - like the warthog and kudu. Then all that is left is the leopard and buffalo; the animals I came to hunt. The ones that beckoned me. I got the buffalo. So here I am, having collected a number of animals I did not really care about; but the main one I came for has evaded me.

The INNER FORCE

I remember the first bear I killed was on the twenty-first day - the **last** day of the season. It was **last** light. My mountain lion was harvested on the **last** day at dusk. My grizzly bear was down on the sixteenth day, which was the **last** day. All of them predators, all of them packed into camp around midnight the **last** day.

Is that what this hunt was meant to be? My mind is full of doubts and questions that are becoming continuously clearer. Everything happens for a reason. The Great Maker has a plan. I am a pawn and this is not a coincidence, a quirk of fate. The leopard I shot last night was meant to be. It was his plan for it to die in the dark. It is his plan for me to do more. His intent that my part be bigger in altering the balance of nature. It is not a coincident that I only have one bullet left. It is a preplanned thing, a challenge to me. It is destiny. It could be no other way. The opportunity to hunt in Africa is like being able to play in the World Series, an honor. This series has gone the distance. It is the seventh game. It is the bottom of the ninth. There are two outs with a man on first. We are down by one and I am in the batter's box.

I suddenly know that this game will not go down to the last night. I will be called to bat tonight. If I could lay my money down on the long odds against me right now, I would. And I am not a gambler! It would not be a gamble because as I write this, everything has come to me...everything is perfectly clear. I am positive that I will not have to wait too long. Another leopard will come tonight. This game will end sometime before the sun rises. I will have my shot, my last shot, my chance to send a sliding fast ball deep over the right field fence or strike out and be left with great memories - great, but bitter memories.

We will have to leave for the blind soon, and I am positive that tonight is the night. I predict a cat will come. My chance at a big tom was not meant to be. I believe this will be an average cat. It will be late, perhaps midnight. All this cannot be accidental. It was preplanned by a greater power. It is my will to make a cat appear tonight and I feel it within myself. I can't really explain it. I just now know this is how it is meant to be.

Finally it's time to go to the blind and wait for the sun to sink into the western horizon. Wait for blackness to engulf the moonless African sky! To motionlessly sit and slowly age like freshly made wine on a shelf, waiting for the right time to be uncorked.

June 13 - The Inner Force

It's sunny and warm this morning. Thirteen is my lucky number! Forty-five years and nine months ago today I uttered my first cries on this earth. My mother surely would never have thought her baby would be in Africa today - in the company of other people, another race, another culture. A place where there are no televisions, telephones, or radios. This is a place that is just about living day-to-day.

The rest of the world seems far away and irrelevant. I think I enjoy the solitude the most. These people have little or nothing, but seem to enjoy the pleasures of each new day. They do not race through their lives, filling up time with worries and problems. They do not bother themselves with the trivial bullshit we watch on television and listen to on the radio. For the most part they just enjoy life. And I must say that I enjoy sharing their company. Their carefree attitude is contagious. I find myself looking forward to their companionship more and more. Three cheers for the simple life! Hip-Hip-Hoorah!

Last night made me a prophet of sorts since my prediction has come to pass. I knew yesterday afternoon that against all odds, I would be called to bat. However, my chance came earlier than expected. The time was 7:30 PM.

If you believe in yourself, then success and luck are sure to follow. People who doubt themselves and their capabilities will freeze and panic in a crisis. People who doubt themselves will buy lottery tickets and think maybe they could be lucky. But luck is mostly a reflection of hard work, determination and self-confidence. If you are one of the majority that feels you only have bad luck, then you will. If you are waiting for the golden goose to shit a golden egg in your lap, it is not going to happen.

I have been accused of being lucky all my life. So much that I call my outfitting business LocKey U, which means 'lucky you.' Nobody takes notice when you fall on your face. Oh, it is just a "write-off" they will say. The write-off usually means that you go to work everyday, sometimes for months, trying to recoup the lost income.

Luck is something you make for yourself. Luck is a reflection of hard work, sacrifice and going the extra mile; not giving up. If you think you are not lucky, it is because you have decided on your own that you are a loser. You do not believe in yourself. You are lost and it is too bad that you don't want to be lucky, but picked lazy instead. A person cannot waste his time going through life hoping and waiting for luck. To wish for luck almost certainly will deny you of ever fulfilling your dreams!

Forget about hoping for luck or wishing for luck, but don't stop dreaming! Most importantly, don't be afraid to chase your dreams because that is when dreams become reality. Let the non-dreamers consider you lucky even though luck had nothing to do with your hard-earned success!

A highly educated individual, who regarded himself as a psychiatrist, once told me that dreams are a reflection of wishes. This pathetically lost individual did not understand that dreams are what drive the wheels of free enterprise. Dreams are the advantage of a free society over socialism, communism, or a dictatorship. Every person deserves the opportunity to reach for or seek their dreams. That is called freedom. Thomas Edison and Albert Einstein were dreamers. Wishes are self-destructive and therefore are not a dream; as a dream is not a wish!

"I wish I was a millionaire" translates into the possibility of blowing every penny you have at a casino reaching for a star you cannot touch! I wish I were young, beautiful, strong, handsome, debonair, articulate, athletic, political, and business-minded. I wish I had endurance, stamina, nerves or resolve. Everybody wants to wish for something they do not have and cannot possess.

A wish is not a reflection of a dream because a wish probably will never come true, but a dream can! We have control of our dreams and destiny. We can **make** dreams come true! It takes imagination to dream. It takes courage to reach for a dream. It takes determination, commitment and sacrifice to try and create a dream. It takes unrelenting hard work and leadership to make a dream come true. With desire, dreams become reality. So let your imagination flow and make your dreams come true.

We all have the qualities inside of us to realize a dream, yet some dreams just were not meant be. If and when you fail, you must pick yourself up and try again. That's life!

There was no rumble in the jungle, instead it was quiet. No breeze, no crickets singing, no nothing. It was the calm before the storm. Then the slightest breeze whispered through the trees, leaves fluttered as subtle, soft noise began to awaken the night air. A cricket called out and a varmint of some sort squawked.

The INNER FORCE

The creatures of the night were awakening. My eyes stared into blackness as I scanned the darkness with my ears

I imagined a leopard prowling in the underbrush, carefully and slowly approaching our little trap. I wondered when my dream would become reality, hoping it would be sooner instead of latter. Wishing there was an easier way instead of the agonizing motionless sitting.

As I started to say it was 7:30 PM. It was dark, total darkness. Sitting in quiet, motionless darkness gives you time to think; to evaluate; to look into yourself.

As I gaze into this black empty, yet wondrous forbidding and interesting place, I can't help but reflect on why I do this! Why do I hunt? Why do I risk financial stability, health and even life to go to the far corners of the earth in crazy quests of the unknown? Wasn't marrying and having children at a young age challenging enough? Didn't starting a building business wet my appetite for adventure? Wasn't throwing caution to the wind to risk being self-employed and forging my own path exciting enough? Isn't time to sit back and smell the roses? What compels me to risk and adventure?

Perhaps it is my lack of fear or lack of brains that allows me to ride off into new canyons and drainages without fear of being lost. Or, the bold self-confidence that makes it possible for me to guide men on horseback in total darkness and "feel" the trail where we are going. This lack of fear has always made me wild and willing to go forth without worry. It also allows me to become bored easily. Success bores me. Wealth bores me...not at first, but after awhile if it does not grow, develop and change, it bores me.

Only my beautiful wife has never bored me. Thank God for her! I think that I constantly seek new life when I'm trying to escape the grasp of boredom that compels me to adventure. Adventure is life itself. If you can look into the face of danger and be excited, then for damned sure you are **alive**! To exist without being alive is merely waiting to wither away and die. It is far better to be alive for a short time than to live a long time without being alive. So from this viewpoint, one has little to lose in risk. Risk is a big part of success, of realizing your dreams. Sometimes it is better to throw caution to the wind, take risks, and create your own luck; build your dreams.

We had been silently sitting in the blind. I had programmed myself for a long haul. It had been dark for two hours now. The

Frank Schmitz

stars shined brightly and there was no moon - just like the other night. Just blackness. If this leopard returned, I figured he would pad around our blind as he had done last time, just feet from us, before going to the bait. I knew we would have to be extra quiet. I sat more still than I have done before. The desire was stronger in me. The night was silent except for a few crickets singing their love songs.

I was in a semi-trance, consumed with the thought of the great films of the world; two legged as well as four. A male's mind is a simple devise and it does not take much to keep mine occupied. I could go to jail for some of my thoughts!, but that is another story.

Nixon pokes me. I come to full awareness. I haven't heard a thing — not like the other times. But Nixon has heard the sound of tearing flesh. There is a cat on the bait, a careful cat, a very quiet cat. I ready myself. I had balanced my gun in a position aimed at the left side of the bait, where I expected a leopard to sit and eat. The light goes on. As my eyes struggle to adjust from total darkness to light - I see nothing!

Nixon whispers, "Take him." My eyes look to the right of the bait as Nixon demands again, "Take him Frank!" I think he must be on the ground and look to the ground as Nixon says, "He is standing up behind the bait. Shoot him!" Each instant is a strike against me in this race against time. Then I see him. His body stretching upward, belly facing me, his head hidden by the bait on which he is carefully feasting.

I am sad to say that I do not remember the rest. I aim and my last bullet was on its way at the center of the animal directed at its chest. This is the time we all wait for--we all dream about-- the chance at glory. The seventh game of the World Series. The score is two to three in their favor, the bottom of the ninth, and the count is full. This is your one chance to be immortalized, even if it is only for the audience in your head. It is you against your mind, against your ego. It is a test of mind over matter, will over skill. A test to bring yourself to the next level! It is one chance against all odds, but you control your destiny—win, lose, or draw! It is your chance at personal glory and mind over matter- even if it is only for the audience that is in yourself.

My sweaty hands tightly grip the base of the hickory bat that slowly hovers over my right shoulder. My cleated left foot is firmly planted in the dirt ahead of my body as I stare into the eyes of the

The INNER FORCE

pitcher. He stares past me at the catcher crouched behind, me, reading his call. His head shakes off the first sign and then nods to the second. Their plan is set as he winds back on his right foot and delivers the pitch with all the power locked within his body. The circular projectile rockets towards me at ninety miles per hour. I have only a split second to react. I think it is a fast ball coming in just above my waist as I start my swing.

The adrenaline rush hits me as forty thousand screaming fans rise to their feet, the balance of the game hangs in the next "nano" second. My bat is swinging towards the incoming fast ball, but it is not a fast ball! It's a sinker! The ball begins to dive and instinctively I struggle to react — to swing lower! Now the adrenaline has taken over, the forty thousand people are silent; the ball slowly floats in front of me! The world grinds to a halt as time momentarily stands still. Instinctively, I adjust. Then there is the smacking sound of leather hitting hardwood, a Louisville slugger trying to rip the rawhide off a hard ball. The explosion.... the impact sending this projectile towards its preconceived target. Now the hardball is rocketing deep towards right field, climbing as it goes, gaining momentum. There is the animated face of a broadcaster screaming into his microphone. "I don't believe it. The ball is going, going, it's out of here! The game is over!" Hysteria returns to the crowd as time marches on!

In another time, another place, a different hemisphere, perhaps a different dimension the same theme is playing out, yet it's a different game. The only question that remains is will he strike out, fly out or connect? If you have come to play-- win, lose or draw--you have accomplished more than the forty thousand spectators that fill a stadium. They will cheer you or boo you. They will draw their own conclusions. They can build you up or tear you down, but you still have to play to win. The rest they will judge, they will condemn you or hoist you upon their shoulders. But they cannot lose...because they will not take the chance to win! They are not players. Only players can rise up to be winners. My daughter, Angie, came home from school when only in the fourth grade and said to me one day, "I am rubber, you are glue, what you say to me bounces off me and sticks to you!" That seemingly childless statement is loaded with winner wisdom. It separates the playmaker from the spectators.

Nixon's voice still echo's in my ears "shoot him" even though it was a soft whisper. My eye is focused into the scope of the

Frank Schmitz

416. My last bullet chambered and ready to go. The soft subtle reflection of a white belly speckled in black is upwardly stretched below the hindquarter of raw flesh it feeds upon - illuminated by the spotlight and silhouetted by the darkness behind it. My mind is racing faster and faster, until all that was a rapid blur suddenly screeches to a halt. The next split second stretches slowly towards eternity as the cross hairs in the weapon's optics center on the beast like a piece of hardwood being drawn towards the incoming hardball. There is an explosion, the impact sending a projectile towards its preconceived target!

The stars have come together; the prearranged date with destiny has come to pass! The leopard lay below the bait on the ground, paralyzed with his back broken. The last shot — my final bullet had found its path. Without time to think I had shot at the center of his chest. Was it luck, or was it preplanned destiny that made the bullet exit through his spine?

I do know this. The entire episode lasted just seconds. It was a race against time! Physical reaction of man and beast! No time to second guess the shot. Only the fraction of a second needed to react on instinct. The instinct that allows you to subconsciously pinpoint your target while directing your body to carry out a reflex that sends your mental intention along with a physical projectile to the same spot - "The Inner Force."

It is the same fraction of a second a ball player has when he sees a ball coming towards him at ninety miles an hour. Can he wait to swing until the ball is there at his side? No! He begins to swing in anticipation of his bat meeting that ball when it reaches him, his eyes directed to the spot where he wants that ball to go! At the instant of connection he already knows if it is bleacher bound or a pop-up; his great concentration and inner strength are the reason he succeeds. That is the difference between a batboy and Babe Ruth!

I walked up to the cat to admire his beauty. I was not surprised, because somehow I had known he was a young male, not an old cat. Young, and he was mine. He was meant for me and I am thankful. Yet, as I looked at him I felt sorry for him. I wondered why his destiny was not for a longer time on this earth to let him do what leopards do. Why not send his father or grandpa? I was wondering 'why,' as we do in our own lives when young people are called to their maker. Why so young, when there is so much ahead of them. I guess we will understand in another place and time. I do not know why he was chosen for me, but I do know that it happened for a reason — in a bigger picture that we do not understand.

Yet I am grateful that I have gotten to walk this path, to have felt the inner force, and to have understood it...to know that the belief and power inside you, in your soul, will guide you to good things. You just have to believe in what you want. Believe in your capabilities and the old saying, "Man can move mountains" is true. It is your sixth sense, your instinct, something we often ignore because it is not logical or material. It is why I am not a great shot, but perhaps a great shooter. A great shot researches his equipment and ammo, analyzes, practices, and has proven concepts for everything. It is the guy who you send to the Olympics to drop bullets in a bull's eye at 800 yards.

Me, I am lucky to hit a bull in his ass at 50 yards if I think too much about it. But a shooter pulls up and shoots without thinking; without analyzing. It is a reaction. He does not worry about how to lead, how to hold, wind drift, and angle because he sends the bullet to its target by his instincts, his heart and soul. You do not remember anything except the feeling in yourself when it was the right instant to pull the trigger. It comes from belief in yourself, survival instincts if you will. It comes from being at peace with yourself and understanding your place in the big picture - knowing that you are following your destiny. What happens is for a reason, so you have no reason not to believe in yourself and in the inner force!

I gaze upon the beautiful spotted beast that lies peacefully at my feet. I admire this wonderful animal for his stealthy strength and freedom. I am sad the long quest is over, as I realize he represents all that I admire and respect. I hope that part of his spirit will stay with me and that part of mine will stay with him.

Frank Schmitz

For twenty years, I owned and ran my own construction company. The first years we struggled, doing whatever had to be done to raise our girls. I bartended, split wood and never let pride get in the way of providing. Later I became modestly successful financially (upper middle class I would say), but we had money to do what we wanted.

However, the stress and burden of running my business took a toll. To maintain our lifestyle, I often had to sacrifice family, putting business first. That was the price I had to pay if we wanted to enjoy the monetary rewards. I worked long hard hours in the field during the day and doing bidding and billing, etc. at night. With success comes demand. The phone never stopped ringing. It started to torment me; people calling morning, noon and night--seven days a week--the constant hounding coming to my house, even on Sundays and holidays. I was a prisoner to my own success. My escape was hunting in distant lands and places - seeking solitude. I wanted to be inaccessible; with nature; and loved every moment of it.

The INNER FORCE

My first great big hunt was in northern British Columbia, hundreds of miles from a road on horseback. It was winter and cold. One morning it was eighteen degrees in my tent. The tent was bottomless and we slept on pine branches. I realized, this is what I enjoy; this is when I fell in love with the backcountry. I did not want to leave. I even dabbled around a couple of extra days while my business hung in the balance. I did not want to go home to the world - to the life most of us live; a mad rush - a fast, one lane race to our deaths.

For half a year, Terri worried about me as I would sit in my game room watching and re-watching the video we had made. My heart had stayed in the mountains and kept calling to me until one day, through luck or destiny, my chance was right to throw caution to the wind; sell my business and properties; and move to the mountains.

I am now busier than ever operating my outfitting business and our lodge and store (among other things)., But we have a ranch and animals; and **we enjoy life**. We live day to day. I often do not see television for months on end. But I was not sure until now, sitting here in Africa, if I had escaped the strangle hold of being alive but not living.

I look to the night sky; at stars in an endless universe; at eternity. I am **alive**. I have played. I have wallowed in the despair of losing and rejoiced in the sweet taste of victory. But for the first time ever, I am tired of being away. I am ready and want to go home. I want to be with my wife, return to my ranch, and enjoy the companionship of my dogs and horses until the next challenge beckons me.

I have felt the inner force and found the inner peace. I am a lucky man indeed!

In closing:

Well, as Paul Harvey would say....."And now for the rest of the story!"

Like a never-ending story, a strange twist of fate has called me to bat in a much bigger game than I wanted to play in. Like the challenge of some hunts, this game is for life or death. But, unlike the hunt, I have less control over my destiny. My maker stands on the mound, the grim reaper is the catcher, and I stand between them - wondering if I can hit safely or will strike out.

When I wrote this story I thought my health problems had been conquered. Unfortunately, the disease attacked again, rupturing veins in my feet, leaving me temporarily crippled. After many mistrials, I finally was diagnosed with Vasculitis; a non-curable disease brought on by a break down in your auto immune system. This breakdown was brought on by another non-curable disease called Wegners Granulomatosis. Our new goal or lease on life is called 'remission.' This is the new game I play. My defense is called chemotherapy and prednisone - the scary sounding tools to remission.

But, the game is not as bad as it sounds **because I cannot lose. I will win.** It may change or limit my physical capabilities, but, as I've stated before, things happen for a reason. The worst-case scenario is my maker comes calling. I will go serve for I have no regrets in my life...nothing to look back on - only to look forward. The will to live beckons strongly. That alone defies the grim reaper.

Mother Nature calls to me, as does "Old Lady Africa." Already the force from within is calling me back to the Dark Continent. The desire to do the tango with African lions and elephants beckon me. There is also the mighty Kodiak bear and the majestic Marco Polo rams of Mongolia. Perhaps with my legs jeopardized they have a chance! Ah, but so do I! It must all be part of the master plan.

The master plan obviously challenges me. The road I have traveled went from a dirt trail; to a footpath; leading eventually to a gravel road; then to black top; until I sped along on a super-highway. I traveled there with ease; going too fast on a smooth road until I decided it was time to slow down and smell the roses. I took the side road and enjoyed the ride. But the road has turned rougher and bumpier than expected. I will have to go into four wheel drive and then to four hoof drive as the mountain becomes steep and rugged. Now I ride forth on a treacherous mountainous trail with new challenges and new adventures that lie ahead. I do not ride along seeking the end of the trail, however I seek the beginning.

    I expect to see many sun rises and hope to experience many seasons in my search for the beginning of the eternal quest.

    The maker is now winding up to hurl the next pitch. I stare back at him griping my hard wood bat tightly knowing that it is a moment for time to stand still. My palms are not sweaty because I am not nervous. Now the pitch is being delivered and soon hard wood will meet rawhide sending the projectile to its preconceived destination. I will be safe..., that is the power of "The Inner Force".

"The End"

To order additional copies of "The Inner Force", signed by the author go to www.lockeyu.com

What is your color?
If roses are really red
And violets are really blue
Than what color describes the sky
What will we do?
If tulips are bright yellow
But so is a cowardly fellow
If a plants new foliage is brilliant green
Than what color is greed or is it just mean?
If coal is described as the color of black
Does that mean we can take a bad day back?
But than perhaps if mother natures milk is white
Than we can rest assured all things are all right!
Even though all the colors in a rainbow are not clear
Our lives can carry on- transparent but without fear
You see it is not the color of our skin.
Nor the color that lies within
It is our chance to be on this earth
That we have a chance to create a color for whatever its worth
So once we have passed on into this ground
Perhaps a new color than can be found.

Frank Schmitz
9/13/03
My favorite color is hunter green!